Men-at-Arms • 450

American Loyalist Troops 1775–84

René Chartrand • Illustrated by G & S Embleton
Series editor Martin Windrow

First published in Great Britain in 2008 by Osprey Publishing,
Midland House, West Way, Botley, Oxford OX2 0PH, UK
44-02 23rd St, Suite 219, Long Island City, NY 11101, USA

Email: info@ospreypublishing.com

© 2008 Osprey Publishing Ltd.

All rights reserved. Apart from any fair dealing for the purpose of private study, research, criticism or review, as permitted under the Copyright, Designs and Patents Act, 1988, no part of this publication may be reproduced, stored in a retrieval system, or transmitted in any form or by any means, electronic, electrical, chemical, mechanical, optical, photocopying, recording or otherwise, without the prior written permission of the copyright owner. Enquiries should be addressed to the Publishers.

ISBN: 978 1 84603 314 8

Editor: Martin Windrow
Page layouts: Alan Hamp
Index by Glyn Sutcliffe
Originated by United Graphic
Printed in China through World Print Ltd.

10 11 12 13   12 11 10 9 8 7 6 5 4 3

A CIP catalog record for this book is available from the British Library

FOR A CATALOG OF ALL BOOKS PUBLISHED BY OSPREY MILITARY
AND AVIATION PLEASE CONTACT:

Osprey Direct, c/o Random House Distribution Center,
400 Hahn Road, Westminster, MD 21157
E-mail: uscustomerservice@ospreypublishing.com

Osprey Direct, The Book Service Ltd, Distribution Centre,
Colchester Road, Frating Green, Colchester, Essex, CO7 7DW
E-mail: customerservice@ospreypublishing.com

www.ospreypublishing.com

Author's note

This study of American provincial Loyalist units tries to present an account of the corps that gathered those American men – and women, by extension – who chose to remain loyal to their king, and to fight to maintain what they perceived as their legitimate government. They were on the losing side, and their choice cost them everything they had, eventually sending the survivors into exile in their tens of thousands. Shunned or despised by most American historians, the Loyalists became legendary heroes in the country they so deeply transformed – Canada – and, to a lesser extent, in the Bahamas.

Sources cited in the text

References in brackets to AO (Audit Office), CO (Colonial Office), PRO (Public Records Office), T (Treasury) and WO (War Office) refer to series at the National Archives (formerly Public Records Office) at Kew, London, UK. Those with the reference Add Mss are from the British Library in London. See also introductory note to Select Bibliography, page 39.

Acknowledgments

The material in this book is the result of many years of research into the various aspects surrounding Loyalist provincial corps, notably their actual services and their material culture. Fellow historians and friends have been most helpful: Francis Back, Brian Dunnigan, Don Graves, James Kochan, Don Troiani and Gavin Watts; the late Albert W. Haarmann; the late W.Y. Carman; and Gerry Embleton, whose talent for recreating the 18th century graces the color plates for this monograph.

Artist's note

Readers may care to note that the original paintings from which the color plates in this book were prepared are available for private sale. All reproduction copyright whatsoever is retained by the Publishers. For more information, visit:

www.gerryembleton.com

The Publishers regret that they can enter into no correspondence upon this matter.

TITLE PAGE **Standard of the King's American Dragoons, c.1782–83.** The standards were presented to the regiment at New York in early August 1782. The silk field was dark blue (now discolored to a greenish shade), with scarlet circular backgrounds for the central and four corner badges embroidered in gold, silver, and natural-colored threads for the various floral and heraldic devices, including the tree crest above the central device. The corner badges are alternating rose-and-thistle sprays, and white horses. The central badge has the letters "LD," for Light Dragoons, on a circular blue ground in a star with gilt rays. The scroll reads "The King's American Dragoons," embroidered and edged in gold on the dark blue field. (New Brunswick Museum, St John; author's photo)

AMERICAN LOYALIST TROOPS 1775–84

INTRODUCTION

THE AMERICAN WAR OF INDEPENDENCE or Revolutionary War fought between 1775 and 1783 was, in some respects, a civil war. From the very first engagements in 1775, there were Americans who supported the actions of the British government in its American colonies, and who were opposed to any unilateral measures by their fellow citizens that would result in independence from the mother country. These Americans became known as the "Loyalists," from their loyalty to Great Britain, its king and its government. Open supporters of the Loyalist cause were in a minority, but not a negligible one; it may be estimated at about 20 per cent of the population living in the original "Thirteen Colonies" at the time of the American Declaration of Independence in 1776. They came from all walks of life and origins; most were of British descent, but some were Indians, and others were African Americans. Furthermore, there were many individuals who took the side of the British Crown outside the borders of the original colonies. These were inhabitants of the provinces of Nova Scotia, Prince Edward Island, Newfoundland, East and West Florida, and – most of all – the province of Québec (which encompassed much of present-day central Canada, and was often simply called "Canada" at that time). Further away, Jamaica in the British West Indies received Loyalist units from North America to fight the Spanish in Central America.

An important point to note was the division of North America into two separate command areas, ordered by the Earl of Dartmouth on August 2, 1775, and probably effective by the fall of that year. One command (essentially present-day Québec and Ontario) was under the governor of Canada, Sir Guy Carleton; the other, under General Gage and his successors, embraced the present Canadian Atlantic provinces and the American colonies on the seaboard (CO 42/34). This division had an important impact on Loyalist corps: each of these commands represented a different troop establishment and supply system, which has understandably confused some historians unaware of this administrative detail. Orders and supplies destined for a corps serving in the Canadian command came under a different authority from those for a corps in New York. Thus a corps such as the King's Royal Regiment of New York was in fact, in spite of its name, part of the Canadian establishment. As the supply network was also different, assumptions that uniforms and arms sent to New

Officer said to be Col James De Lancey, leader of De Lancey's Refugees in 1776; however, his uniform appears to be that of the 2nd Battalion of Oliver De Lancey's Brigade, raised later. It agrees with the description in the 1783 North American Army List from New York: a red coat with plain blue lapels, and buttons set in pairs. The buttons and epaulettes were silver. (Print after portrait; Anne S.K. Brown Military Collection, Brown University, Providence, USA; author's photo)

York would be issued to units in Canada cannot be sustained. (See also the passages under "Uniforms" on pages 41–42.) Furthermore, due to distance and the slow and limited means of communication, colonies such as Newfoundland or West Florida tended to be semi-autonomous commands. Finally, some American Loyalist corps were sent to serve further afield, in Bermuda, the Bahamas, Jamaica and Central America, all areas which fell under other commands.

To define exactly who was a Loyalist, and if a provincial unit raised on the American continent falls into that category, thus becomes a hazardous and somewhat futile exercise. The fundamental factor common to all was that they rallied to fight for the British Crown. Their reasons were extremely varied: some were part of the British government's social and political establishment in America, others had strong business ties with Britain, and still others felt that their rights would be better protected by the Crown than by the rampaging advocates of "Liberty," who in practice often turned violently upon anyone who disagreed with their arguments.

Indeed, quite early in the conflict, the more passionate promoters of independence brutally persecuted their loyal or "Tory" neighbors, and seized their property. This treatment created sizeable groups of bitter refugees, who demanded arms and the means to create corps to fight for the Crown in the American colonies; and as early as the middle of 1775 the first units of Loyalist volunteers started to appear in Boston, Nova Scotia and Québec. For their part, the British authorities gladly sanctioned these units of "Royal Provincial" troops, created specific provincial military establishments for them, and supplied money, arms, uniforms and logistical assistance. Soon, every North American province would have them. As the conflict expanded, the movement to create provincial units loyal to the Crown also spread. Most Indian nations opted to ally themselves with the British. One could say that the Loyalist movement even exported itself, when such units raised in North America were sent to the West Indies and Central America.

Loyalist contribution

In most cases, the Loyalist corps in North America could provide excellent information on terrain and enemy strength when operating in familiar parts of the country. British senior officers were thus just as well informed in such matters as their American opponents. In tactical terms, many Loyalist corps were meant to be light troops that would manoeuvre swiftly and in loose formation, strike quickly and keep moving. The most famous Loyalist corps – such as the Queen's Rangers, the British Legion and Butler's Rangers – were made up of units of both light infantry and light cavalry. In the case of the Queen's Rangers and

OPPOSITE

MAIN **The main theatres of the American War of Independence, at the turn of 1777–78.**

INSET **Spanish Nicaragua in Central America. During the 18th century the British made many incursions on its Atlantic coast, established outposts, and won the friendship of the Indians on the "Mosquito Coast" (modern Belize – upper right). These became steadfast allies against the Spanish who were settled on the western half of the isthmus, and in April 1780 aided a mixed force of British regulars, Loyalists and volunteers who ventured deep into Spanish territory and captured Fort St Juan. The main British outpost of Bluefields was situated south of Pearl Cay. (Map from Fortescue's *History of the British Army*; author's photo)**

Loyalist light infantry privates in marching order, c.1780. Many Loyalist units were light infantry troops, whose general appearance in the field is reconstructed here by F.P. Todd. Instead of tricorn hats and coats with long tails, light infantrymen wore caps and shortened coats. Short gaiters were standard wear for all troops on campaign, but in America rough linen gaiter-trouser overalls were very popular. In addition to the cartridge box and bayonet scabbard shown, accoutrements might also include a belly cartridge box and a powder horn. Haversacks, knapsacks, blanket rolls and canteens would also be carried. (Anne S.K. Brown Military Collection, Brown University, Providence, USA; author's photo)

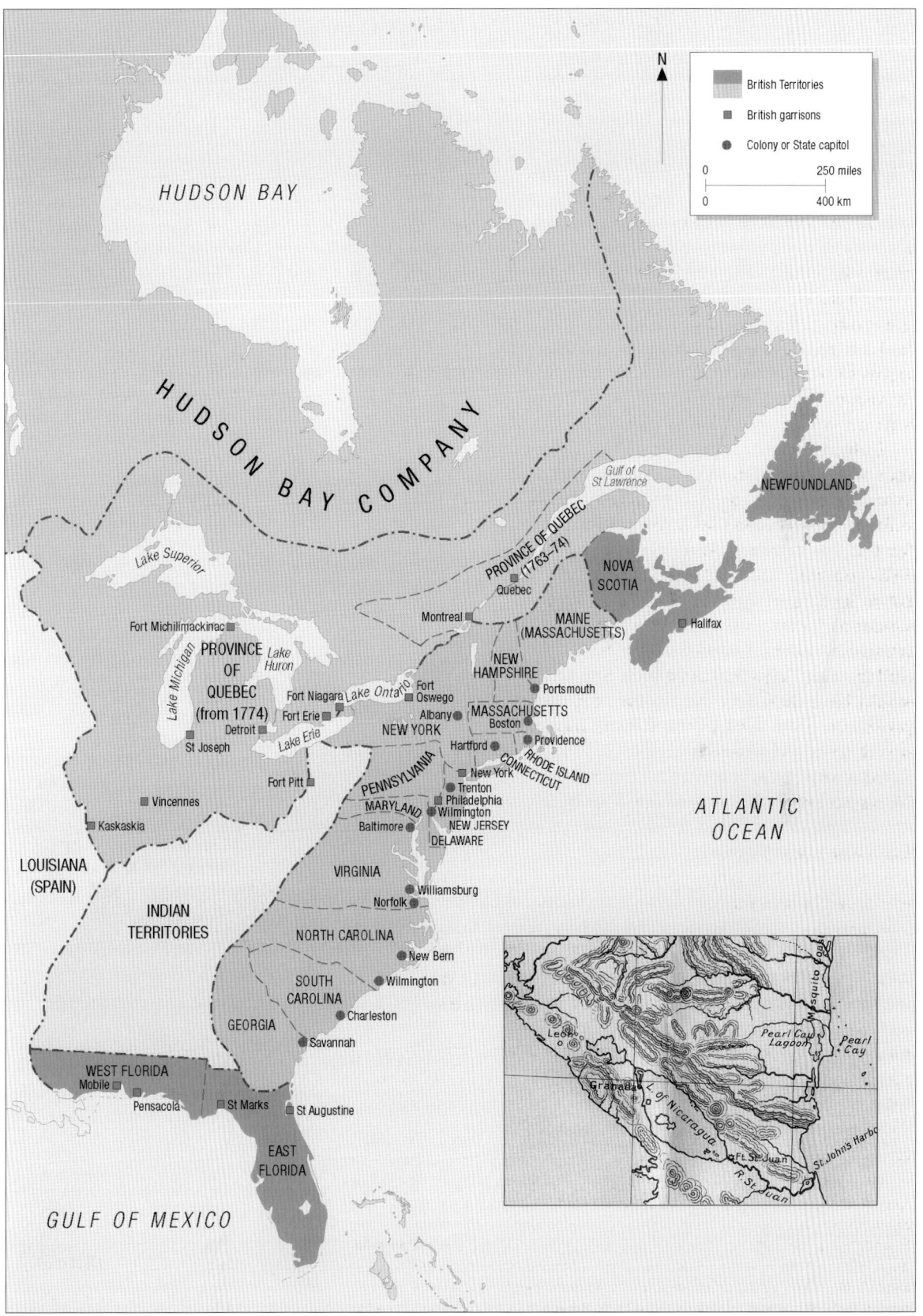

"Thayeadanegea – Joseph Brant, the Mohawk Chief" in 1776, in a portrait made by George Romney during the visit to London by this most influential of all the Loyalist Indian leaders. His headdress has mostly red with some white feathers rising from a black band. Silver rings hang from his hair and onto his right shoulder. The shirt is white, the gorget, cross and arm bracelets silver, over narrow dark brown crossbelts with a silver buckle. A black cloth is wrapped around his waist and over his left shoulder, under a white, green and red cloth at the waist. Blue upper leg wear and red *mitasses* (Indian-style gaiters) cover the knee and thigh. He holds a tomahawk in his right hand. A British officer later described Joseph Brant wearing "moccasins elegantly trimmed with beads, leggins and breech-cloth of superfine blue; short green coat, with two silver epaulets, and a small laced, round hat. By his side hung an elegant silver-mounted cutlass, and his blanket of blue cloth ... was gorgeously decorated with a border of red ..." (National Gallery of Canada, Ottawa; author's photo)

the British Legion, they provided a sizeable and very effective light cavalry and light infantry to a main British army operating in settled American heartlands such as New Jersey, South Carolina or Virginia. Butler's Rangers represented a very different application of light infantry tactics; this corps specialized in raids on wilderness frontier communities in partnership with Indian allies. In this case, the Loyalist frontiersmen replicated almost exactly the practices that had made the settlers of New France and their Indian allies so feared and effective until the surrender of Canada to the British forces in 1760.

However, not all Loyalist light corps achieved such fame and success, and many spent much of their time in garrisons. Most Loyalist units in the American seaboard provinces were meant to act as line infantry; some, such as the Loyal American Regiment or De Lancey's Brigade, were often deployed on campaign or participated in sieges, and gave distinguished service; but others attracted too few recruits for campaign service, and usually served in large garrisons such as the city of New York. At the end of 1778, some 6,300 Loyalist soldiers were spread among 31 units, thus giving an average of 204 men per unit on the Atlantic seaboard. A few corps – such as the Queen's Rangers, the Volunteers of Ireland or the Royal Highland Emigrants – had between 300 and 400 men each, and were considered very effective. The strength of most of the other units hovered between 100 and 200 men, sometimes fewer, and these were thus unable to make any serious contribution (CO 5/96 and 97). In Canada the smaller Loyalist corps were merged into one unit, Jessup's Loyal Rangers, in late 1781; but no such measures were taken on the Atlantic seaboard, so that most Loyalist corps in that region remained understrength and thus less effective than if they had been amalgamated.

British Union flag carried by Indians or Rangers on the raid into the Wyoming Valley in Pennsylvania during July 1778. Indians were especially fond of carrying such flags into battle. Note that before the 1801 Act of Union with Ireland the flag lacked the red saltire overlaying the white saltire of Scotland. (From a print in the *U.S. Military Magazine*, August 1840; author's photo)

LOYALIST PARTICIPATION IN MAJOR ACTIONS

It is naturally impractical, for reasons of space, to list all the many smaller engagements in which Loyalist corps took part. For instance, the militia units of Westchester and Queen's counties, near New York City, were involved in many skirmishes not mentioned here. Nevertheless, even this outline chronology is clear evidence of the important contribution of the Loyalist corps during the Revolutionary War.

1775
April 1775–March 11, 1776, Siege of Boston: Royal Fencible Americans, Loyal American Associators, Loyal Irish Volunteers
September 18–November 2 Siege of St John (Saint-Jean, Québec): Montréal militia
September 24 Skirmish near Montréal (resulting in Ethan Allen's capture): Montréal militia
November 7–12 Siege of Ninety-Six, SC: South Carolina militia
December 6, 1775–May 6, 1776, Siege of Québec by Americans: Québec City Militia, Royal Highland Emigrants
December 9 Great Bridge (near Norfolk, VA): Ethiopian Regt, Queen's Own Loyal Virginia Regt

1776
January 1 Blockade and bombardment of Norfolk, VA: detachments Ethiopian Regt, Queen's Own Loyal Virginia Regt, Virginia militiamen under Lord Dunmore
February 27 Moore's Creek Bridge, NC: Scots Loyalists from North Carolina
May 20 Fort Cedars (now Les Cédres, Québec): Canadian militia, Indians
August 27 Long Island, NY: New York Volunteers
October 28 White Plains, NY: New York Volunteers, Queen's Rangers
November 10–28 Siege of Fort Cumberland (Aulac, New Brunswick): Royal Fencible Americans, militia
November 29 Sortie from Fort Cumberland: Royal Fencible Americans, Royal Highland Emigrants

1777
January 2 Raid on Monmouth Court House, NJ: 2nd New Jersey Volunteers
February 18 Lawrence Neck, NJ: detachments of 1st, 2nd, 3rd & 6th New Jersey Volunteers
April 27–28 Raid on Danbury, CT: Prince of Wales' American Regt, Guides & Pioneers
August 2–6 Fort Stanwix & Oriskany, NY: Butler's Rangers, King's Royal Regt of New York, Iroquois Indians, Canadian militia company
August 22 Staten Island, NY: 1st, 3rd, 4th, 5th & 6th New Jersey Volunteers, Richmond County militia, detachment 2nd New Jersey Volunteers
August 22 Kingsbridge, NY: New York Volunteers, King's American Regt, 2nd De Lancey's Bde
September–October Saratoga battles, NY: Jessup's Rangers (King's Loyal Americans), Queen's Loyal Rangers, McAlpin's Corps, Mackay's Corps, Batteaumen, Canadian companies
September 11 & 26 Brandywine, PA, and occupation of Philadelphia: Queen's Rangers, 2nd New Jersey Volunteers, Guides & Pioneers
October 4 Germantown, PA: Queen's Rangers, 2nd New Jersey Volunteers
October 6 Forts Montgomery & Clinton, NY: Emerich's Chasseurs, Loyal Americans, New York Volunteers

1778
April 8 Smithfield, PA: Philadelphia Light Dragoons, Bucks County Light Dragoons, Queen's Rangers
June 28 Monmouth, NJ: Queen's Rangers, 2nd New Jersey Volunteers, Pennsylvania Loyalists, Maryland Loyalists, Roman Catholic Volunteers, Volunteers of Ireland, Caledonian Volunteers, Philadelphia Light Dragoons, Bucks County Light Dragoons, Guides & Pioneers, Black Pioneers; detachments 3rd New Jersey Volunteers, Emmerich's Chasseurs
July 3–4 Wyoming Valley, PA: Butler's Rangers, Iroquois Indians
August 18 Tioga, PA: Butler's Rangers
August 29 Quaker Hill, RI: King's American Regt
September 23–October 14 Grand Forage, Bergen County, NJ: 4th New Jersey Volunteers, Volunteers of Ireland, Guides & Pioneers
September 28 Old Tappan, NJ: Queen's Rangers, Emerich's Chasseurs
October Raids on New York and Pennsylvania borders: Butler's Rangers
November 11 Cherry Valley, NY: Butler's Rangers, Iroquois Indians
December 28–29 Giradeau's Plantation & British capture of Savannah, GA: New York Volunteers; detachments 1st & 2nd De Lancey's Bde, 3rd New Jersey Volunteers

1779
January 10 Fort Morris, GA: South Carolina Royalists, East Florida Rangers, detachment 3rd New Jersey Volunteers

February 14 Kettle Creek, GA: North Carolina militia

February 23–25 American siege and capture of Fort Vincennes (now IN): Detroit Volunteers, militia

March 3 Briar Creek, GA: South Carolina Royalists, East Florida Rangers, Georgia Light Dragoons; detachments 3rd New Jersey Volunteers, New York Volunteers, 1st & 2nd De Lancey's Bde

June 20 Stono Ferry, SC: South Carolina Royalists, Royal North Carolina Regt

July Raid into Connecticut: King's American Regt

July 16 Stoney Point, NY: detachments Loyal American Regt, Volunteers of Ireland

August 5 New Rochelle, NY: Queen's Rangers, Emmerich's Chasseurs, British Legion, Diemar's Hussars

August 19 Paulus Hook, NJ: detachments 2nd & 4th New Jersey Volunteers, Royal Garrison Battalion

September 15–October 9 Successful British defence of Savannah, GA: 1st & 2nd De Lancey's Bde, 3rd New Jersey Volunteers, New York Volunteers, Georgia Loyalists, Royal North Carolina Regt, South Carolina Royalists, King's (Carolina) Rangers, Georgia Light Dragoons, Black Pioneers of Savannah, militia; detachments British Legion, 4th New Jersey Volunteers, Volunteers of Ireland, Maryland Loyalists

September 21–22 Spanish capture of Baton Rouge and Natchez (West Florida, now MS): local militia

October 26 Raritan, Somerset & Brunswick, NJ: Queen's Rangers, Bucks County Light Dragoons, Stewart's Light Dragoons

1780

January 15–16 Staten Island, NY: Queen's Rangers, Volunteers of Ireland, 1st & 4th New Jersey Volunteers, Stewart's Light Dragoons, Richmond County Militia

March 9–14 Spanish capture of Mobile (West Florida, now AL): local militia

March 20–May 11 British siege and capture of Charleston, SC: Queen's Rangers, Volunteers of Ireland, Prince of Wales' American Regt, New York Volunteers, South Carolina Royalists, Royal North Carolina Regt, American Volunteers, Black Pioneers (of New York & Savannah); detachments 1st De Lancey's Bde, 3rd New Jersey Volunteers, Guides & Pioneers

April 14 Monck's Corner, SC: British Legion, American Volunteers

April 16 Hopper's Town, NJ: Stewart's Light Dragoons, Deimar's Hussars; detachments Queen's Rangers, 4th New Jersey Volunteers, Loyal American Regt

April 29 Spanish surrender of Fort San Juan at southern end of Lake Nicaragua, Central America: Jamaica Volunteers, Jamaica Legion, Royal Batteaux Corps, Independent Mosquito Shore Volunteers

May 26 Attack on St Louis (now MO) repulsed by Spanish: Detroit Volunteers, Indians and Canadians

May 29 Waxhaws, SC: British Legion

June 23 Springfield, NJ: Queen's Rangers, 1st & 4th New Jersey Volunteers; detachments Guides & Pioneers, Deimar's Hussars

July 6–7 Connecticut Farms, NJ: 1st & 4th New Jersey Volunteers; detachments Guides & Pioneers, Deimar's Hussars

July 12 Williamson's Plantation, SC: detachments Volunteers of Ireland, British Legion, South Carolina militia

July 30 Rocky Mount, SC: New York Volunteers, South Carolina militia (Floyd's Regt), detachment British Legion

August 6 Hanging Rock, SC: Prince of Wales' American Regt, Royal North Carolina Regt, detachment British Legion

August 16 Camden, SC: British Legion, Volunteers of Ireland, Royal North Carolina Regt, North Carolina Volunteers, detachment Guides & Pioneers

September 14–18 Siege and relief of Augusta, GA: King's (Carolina) Rangers; detachments 3rd New Jersey Volunteers, 1st De Lancey's Bde, Georgia and South Carolina militia

October 7 King's Mountain, SC: American Volunteers; detachments 1st De Lancey's Bde, 3rd New Jersey Volunteers, South and North Carolina militia

October 16 Destruction of Ballstown, NY: King's Royal Regt of New York

October 19 Stone Arabia Heights & Fort Hendrick's Ford: King's Royal Regt of New York, Butler's Rangers

1781

January 7 Mobile Village, AL: United Corps of Pennsylvania & Maryland Loyalists, West Florida Royal Foresters

January 17 Cowpens, SC: Prince of Wales' American Regt, British Legion

February 1 Tarrant's Tavern/Cowan's Ford, NC: British Legion

February 25 Haw River, NC: British Legion

March 8 near Canty's Plantation, SC: King's

American Regt, Provincial Light Infantry, detachment 2nd Royal Highland Emigrants

March 9–May 10 Spanish siege and capture of Pensacola (West Florida, now FL): United Corps of Pennsylvania & Maryland Loyalists, West Florida Royal Foresters

March 15 Guilford Courthouse, NC: British Legion

April 22–May 4 Natchez (West Florida, now MS): Natchez Volunteers

April 25 Hobkirk's Hill (near Camden, SC): Volunteers of Ireland, New York Volunteers, King's American Regt, South Carolina Royalists, detachments South Carolina Rangers, Provincial Light Infantry

May 22–June 21 Siege of Ninety-Six, SC: 1st & 3rd De Lancey's Bde, detachment South Carolina militia. Relief force: Volunteers of Ireland, New York Volunteers, Provincial Light Infantry, South Carolina Light Dragoons; detachments British Legion, South Carolina Royalists, 1st New Jersey Volunteers, 2nd Royal Highland Emigrants, South Carolina militia

May 23–June 5 Siege of Augusta, GA: detachments 3rd New Jersey Volunteers, South Carolina Volunteers, Georgia Loyalists, West Florida Refugees and Georgia militia

June 26 Spencer's Ordinary, VA: Queen's Rangers, detachment New York Volunteers

June 21–22 Pleasant Valley, SC: 4th New Jersey Volunteers, Loyal American Regt, Stewart's Light Dragoons, detachment 1st New Jersey Volunteers

June 28 Spanish recapture of Natchez: Natchez Volunteers

July 6 Jamestown Ford (Green Springs, VA): British Legion

August 2 Rockfish, NC: Royal North Carolina Regt, North Carolina Light Dragoons

August 20 Newbern, NC: Royal North Carolina Regt, North Carolina Light Dragoons

September 8 Eutaw Springs, SC: 1st De Lancey's Bde, New York Volunteers, New Jersey Volunteers, Provincial Light Infantry, detachment 2nd Royal Highland Emigrants

September 12–13 Hillborough & Lindley Mills, NC: North Carolina militia (Fanning's, McNeil's & McDougall's regts)

September Raid on New London, CT: American Legion

October 6–19 Siege and surrender of Yorktown, VA, to Franco-American army: detachments Queen's Rangers, British Legion, North Carolina Volunteers, Pioneers; small detachments Loyal Foresters, 3rd New Jersey Volunteers, New York Volunteers, King's American Regt, De Lancey's Bde, North Carolina Independent Co, Virginia volunteers and militia

October 25 Johnstown, NY: King's Royal Regt of New York

October 30 Raid on West Canada Creek, NY: Butler's Rangers, King's Royal Regt of New York

1782

January 3 Video's Bridge, SC: Volunteers of Ireland; detachments New York Volunteers, South Carolina Royalists

February 24–25 Santee & Tydiman's (Tiedemann's) Plantation, SC: South Carolina Royalists, South Carolina militia; detachments New York Volunteers, British Legion, King's American Dragoons

May 8 Spanish capture of Nassau, Bahamas: Royal Garrison Bn (2 coys)

May 21 Ogeechee, GA: King's American Regt, King's (Carolina) Rangers, Georgia militia

June 4–5 Sandusky, OH: Butler's Rangers, Indian Department and Indians

July Raids into Mohawk Valley: King's Royal Regt of New York

August 15 & 18 Bryant's Station & Blue Licks, KY: Butler's Rangers, Indian Dept and Indians

August 29 Fair Lawn, SC: North Carolina Light Dragoons, South Carolina Royalists (Light Dragoons), Black Dragoons

August 30 Black River Bluff, Central America: Loyal American Rangers, Black River Volunteers, Mosquito Coast Indians

1783

February 13 Defense of Fort Oswego, NY: King's Royal Regt of New York

April 18 Loyalist recapture of Nassau, Bahamas: South Carolina Loyalist refugees, Bahamas volunteers

UNIT HISTORIES

The short unit histories below were compiled from a great variety of sources, notably the muster rolls and pay lists now preserved at Library and Archives Canada. Data concerning the units' uniforms, where found, are given, but readers are directed to the more detailed discussion on pages 41–47. The most important manuscript sources described on those pages are abbreviated here as "1777 List," "Wiederhold" and "1783 NY List."

The histories are divided into five parts – the 13 Colonies; Canada; Nova Scotia, St John & Newfoundland; East & West Florida; and the West Indies & Central America — which equate roughly to the *de facto* areas of military command.

LtCol Banastre Tarleton, commander of the British Legion, 1782; print after portrait by Sir Joshua Reynolds. He is shown wearing the famous black leather "Tarleton" helmet with its visor, bearskin crest, dark green turban confined by small gilt chains, and a red feather; a dark green jacket with black collar and cuffs, gold buttons and lace; white breeches, black boots with brown tops, and brown sabre belt. (Private collection; author's photo)

THE 13 COLONIES

American Legion Raised and stationed on Long Island, NY, from October 1780; New York area, 1781; Staten Island, 1782–83; commanded by BrigGen Benedict Arnold. Supposed strength above 1,000 all ranks, but actually only about 100 in September 1782, in three cavalry troops and one infantry company (Library of Congress, Ms Division, 6A, Vol.7, British deserter reports). Detachment 6 officers and 29 men at James River, VA, with BrigGen Philip's force in April–May 1781 (T 28/2); raids on Portsmouth, VA, in June 1781, and New London, CT, that September. Last muster roll, August 1783.

American Volunteers (also known as **Ferguson's Detachment**) Organized in New York in late 1779 by Maj Patrick Ferguson, from "picked men" from various provincial units – considered an elite corps. To Charleston, SC, 1780; destroyed that October at King's Mountain, where Ferguson was killed; dispersed thereafter; last pay list February 1781. *Uniform*: The dress of their former units; armed with ordinary muskets and short rifles.

Amherst's Corps – see under West Indies

Armed Boatmen Company raised from July 1781 under Capt William Luce and, in 1783, Nathan Hubbill; served in New York and on lower Hudson River; skirmish at Tom's River, NJ, March 1782; disbanded c.September 1783.

Associated Loyalists Born of a 1780 scheme to organize secretly in American-held areas men who would be "willing and able to bear arms, and desirous to associate themselves," to be "duly enrolled under the command" of officers to fight and serve as guides when British troops appeared in their areas, when they would be armed and supplied. Many loyalists in Maryland and Virginia took the "secret oath"; however, American spies who obtained the names of some officers and privates infiltrated the movement. A June 1781 report stated that some 1,500 Loyalists had been arrested in each state and that some were being tried in American Militia Courts. The Associated Loyalists were thrown "in great confusion" as a result, and vanished soon thereafter (CO 5/102 and 103).

Batteaumen – see under Canada

Black Dragoons Raised in South Carolina in 1782, they served as individuals in troops of Loyalist regiments, notably the South Carolina Royalists. A pay list for a distinct Black Pioneer Troop of 30 dragoons of all ranks under Capt March exists for July 1 to September 30, 1782 (T 50/2). Skirmished with Marion's American troops in August 1782; at least 300 transferred to St Augustine that December. **See South Carolina Royalists**, and **Carolina Corps** under West Indies.

Black Pioneers Company raised in the Carolinas in May 1776 with runaway slaves. To New York and on pay strength from August 1776; to Providence in December; then New York; to Philadelphia in 1778, then New York; to Charleston, December 1779; siege of Charleston; back to New York, summer 1780. Attached to Guides & Pioneers from August 25, 1782; disbanded c.September 1783. *Uniform*: green in 1777.

British Legion Authorized July 28, 1778, under Lord Cathcart, and LtCol Banastre Tarleton from 1779; six troops of light cavalry, four companies of infantry. To Savannah, December 1779; siege of Charleston, 1780, and many other engagements in Southern campaign during which, under Tarleton's outstanding leadership, it became one of the most effective corps of the Crown forces. Mustered 418 all ranks, April 1780 (CO 5/99); on American establishment as **5th American Regt** from March 7, 1781. The infantry of the Legion could ride, and some light artillery might also be used, e.g. when it moved on Waxhaws in May (PRO, 30/55/2784). Most of the Legion was at the siege of Yorktown in October 1781, and interned following surrender; detachments at Charleston and New York merged into the King's American Dragoons. Interned men exchanged and to New York, placed on British establishment on December 25, 1782; six troops in 1783, disbanded that October. *Uniform*: see Plate G.

Buck's County Light Dragoons Raised in Philadelphia from February 1778 under Capt Thomas Sandford, and skirmished in outskirts; to New York with British army in June; attached to Queen's Rangers in 1779, and to British Legion in 1780, merged into the latter in 1782. *Uniform*: Sandford was captured, but escaped wearing a "red coat, trimmed with silver, and nankeen waistcoat and overalls" (*Independent Chronicle*, September 7, 1780).

Caledonian Volunteers Raised in New York from early July 1778 under Capt William Sutherland; merged into British Legion on July 31, 1778.

Chester County Light Dragoons Raised in 1778 under Capt James Jacobs; merged into British Legion later that year.

De Lancey's Refugees Raised during 1776 in Westchester County, near New York, by Col James De Lancey. Its troop of cavalry, about 60 strong, was nicknamed the "Cow-Boys" and also known as the **Westchester Light Horse**; the infantry had a light or "ranger" company among other troops. Skirmished with American troops in the county throughout the war; disbanded in 1783. *Uniform*: The cavalry wore green "with military hats and caps" until about 1781, then scarlet. The light infantry was in green, and the "foot" was not "usually in regular uniform" and wore "all colours," according to veterans (Philip Weaver, *MC&H*, 59, Spring 2007: 50).

De Lancey's Bde Raised from September 1776 under BrigGen Oliver De Lancey in counties adjoining New York; brigade of three 500-man battalions. *1st & 2nd Bns* in capture of Savannah, October 1778; defense of Savannah, September 1779; to South Carolina, December 1779; engagements in Southern campaign, notably Eutaw Springs; *2nd Bn* in Georgia, late 1781. 1st & 2nd Bns merged and renumbered 1st, February 1782, returned to New York that December; *3rd Bn*, which remained in New York, renumbered as 2nd Bn. Disbanded October 1783. *Uniform*: see Plate F.

Diemar's Hussars Troop raised in New York from September 1779, with Brunswick soldiers led by Capt Friedrich von Deimar; on Long Island; to the Queen's Rangers from April 24, 1781; last muster as separate troop in April 1782. *Uniform*: issued black coats, buff coats and some 641 yards of cord, caps, leather breeches, trousers, stockings, boots, greatcoats, pistols and broadswords. The "coats" may have been dolmans and pelisses, trimmed with the cord for a hussar-style uniform (Constance D. Sherman, "Captain Deimar's Regiment of Hussars on Long Island," *Journal of Long Island History*, V, 1965: 1)

Duke of Cumberland's Regt – see under West Indies

East Florida Volunteers – see under East & West Florida

Emmerich's Chasseurs Raised and stationed in New York from April 1776 under LtCol Andreas Emmerich; two troops of light cavalry, three companies of light infantry (of which one rifles). About 250 strong; many men of German origin, since recruiting advertisements in April 1778 in German language, but many deserted. Fought at Fort Clinton, Montgomery and Tappen; ordered disbanded on August 31, 1779. *Uniform*: grey in the 1777 List. Dark brown watch coats and rifles taken by three deserters in February 1778 (NY *Royal Gazette*, February 14, 1778)

Ethiopian Regt (aka **Lord Dunmore's Ethiopian Regt**) Raised from November 1775 at behest of Lord Dunmore, governor of Virginia, from seized African American slaves belonging to American rebels against the Crown. The slaves were promised their freedom in exchange for their service, and the regiment soon had about 200 men led by white Loyalist officers and NCOs. Elements were defeated at Great Bridge near Norfolk, VA, on December 9, 1775. Lord Dunmore's forces remained in the Norfolk area until evacuated to New York in August 1776. The regiment seems to have dissolved at that time, its men being taken into other corps such as a "Virginia Company of Blacks," reported in 1778 as employed as laborers by the Royal Artillery in New York. *Uniform*: see Plate A.

Garrison Battalion – see under West Indies

Georgia Light Dragoons Troop raised in late 1778 under Capt Archibald Campbell, in pay until June 1782.

Georgia Loyalists Regiment authorized at Savannah in May 1779 under Maj James Wright; mustered only 72 all ranks, November 1780; apparently amalgamated into other units,

December 1781, when British evacuated Georgia; does not appear in January 1782 South Carolina returns.

Guides & Pioneers Raised in New York from late 1777 under Maj Samuel Holland, Maj Simon Fraser until 1779, Col Beverly Robinson to 1782, and John Aldingdon; up to five companies. Served in New York area; Philadelphia, March 1778; detachment to South Carolina, late 1779; siege of Charleston, 1780, then to New York; disbanded October 10, 1783. *Uniform:* red (1777 List); red faced with blue indicated for "Pioneers" and faced with black for "Carpenters" on map of Paulus Hook of July 24, 1778; "Red Short Coat, Lappel the Same – Black Cuff & Collar" (1783 NY List).

Hierlihy's Corps of Independent Companies – see under Nova Scotia

King's American Dragoons Raised from February 1781 under LtCol Benjamin Thompson (later Lord Rumford); served in New York area; six troops, four reported mounted in August 1782; reached establishment strength of 60 men per troop that summer. Detachment to South Carolina engaged at Santee and Tydiman's Plantation, February 1782; back in New York by 1783; regiment reported "completely appointed" with "Field Pieces with their Harness, &c., complete for a Troop of Flying Artillery" in March 1783 (WO 1/13); mustered 332 all ranks in April; disbanded October 10, 1783 (CO 5/111). *Uniform:* see Plate G.

King's American Regt Raised from December 1776 in New York under Col Edmund Fanning; 500 men in ten companies including grenadiers and light infantry. Defense of Newport, RI, July 1778; back to New York, summer 1779; to South Carolina, December 1780; in Georgia, June 1781–July 1782 – troop of dragoons raised in Georgia attached to regiment during summer 1781, troop mustered 63 all ranks under Capt Isaac Atwood at Savannah, April 1782. Regiment returned to New York by January 1783; disbanded October 10, 1783. Uniform: see Plate H.

King's (Carolina) Rangers Raised 1779 and on pay from June under LtCol Thomas Brown (or Browne); aka **King's Rangers** (NB not to be confused with Robert Rogers' King's Rangers, serving in Canada and Nova Scotia); ten companies. Initially at Savannah, later Augusta, where it fought on September 16, 1780; Savannah from fall 1781; Charleston from July 1782, until its 240 all ranks evacuated to St Augustine in November 1782; last muster there in June 1783. *Uniform:* "Green Short Coat – Crimson cuff & Collar, Lappel Same as Coat, Plain" (1783 NY List); red coats, no facing or button color indicated (Wiederhold).

King's Orange Rangers – see under Nova Scotia
King's Rangers (Rogers') – see under Canada
Loyal American Rangers – see under West Indies
Loyal American Regt Raised and served in New York City from April 1777 under Col Beverly Robinson, posted in Harlem; to Mount Morris, June 1778; Flushing Fly, August; Harlem, December; Verplank's Point, August 1779; Bloomingdale, November; New York City, June 1780; Long Island, June 1781; Little Bloomingdale, August; McGowan's Pass, September; Flushing Fly, November; Brooklyn, May 1782; Bedford Heights, July; New York City from September until disbandment in 1783. *Uniform:* green (1777 List). "Red Coat, Buff Lappel Plain" (1783 NY List). Red coats faced with green, gold buttons for officers (Wiederhold). A miniature of an officer shows a scarlet coat faced with green (*Acadiensis*, VII, 1907: 30). Col Robinson's portrait shows a scarlet coat with a very dark black-green or blue-black collar and lapels, gold buttons (no lace) and epaulettes.

Loyal Foresters Raised in New York, April 1781, under LtCol John Connally, and posted at Long Island; had only one company; detachment to Virginia to recruit, but commander captured, replaced by Capt Alexander McDonald. Last muster roll, March 1782.

Loyal Newport Associators Company raised in Newport, RI, during 1777 under Capt Simon Pease, Joseph Durfee from January 1778.

Loyal New Englanders Unit raised at Newport, RI, from April 1777 under LtCol George Wightman; to have three companies; said to have had 127 "deserters and refugees" in May 1778, and had only 58 men by July 1779. In New York from December 1779, last muster in October 1781 (LAC, MG23, D1/24). *Uniform:* referred to as a "small regiment of greencoats" by American Gen John Sullivan in May 1778.

Loyal Rhode Islanders Raised from March 1777 at Newport, RI, under Col Edward Cole; one company; last pay June 1778.

Maryland Loyalists Raised in Philadelphia from October 1777 under LtCol James Chalmers; to have eight 60-man companies. To New York in 1778, then to Pensacola via Jamaica that October. Formed part of temporary United Corps of Pennsylvania & Maryland Loyalists at Pensacola from December 1779; distinct unit again after Pensacola's surrender to Spanish, May 1781. Sent to New York from Havana, Cuba, July 1781; officially exchanged on July 24, 1782; served in New York area; last muster December 1783. *Uniform:* "Red Coats – Olive Lappel white button

Troopers of the British Legion as shown in a small image below one of Tarleton's portrait prints published in London's *Westminster Magazine* on April 1, 1782; many details are obviously questionable, but helmets are shown. This is one of the few images showing a Loyalist unit published at the time of the war. (Anne S.K. Brown Military Collection, Brown University, Providence, USA; author's photo)

hole" (1783 NY List). Red coats faced with green, no button color indicated for officers (Wiederhold).

Military Batteaumen – see under East & West Florida

Nassau Blues Unit raised on Long Island, NY, from June 1779 under Col William Axtell – may have been militia, had only about 60 men and disbanded that December. *Uniform:* none known, but name may indicate blue coats.

New Hampshire Volunteers – see **Stark's Corps**

New Jersey Volunteers Large unit raised from September 1776 under BrigGen Cortland Skinner; initially up to six numbered battalions, reduced to five June 1778, four June 1779, three from June 1781 to disbandment. Battalions had variable number of companies in 1777: 1st Bn seven companies, 2nd Bn eight, 3rd Bn six, 4th Bn eight, 5th Bn five, and 6th Bn four – some variations thereafter. All battalions in New Jersey until evacuation in June 1777 to New York. Thereafter, *1st Bn* served in New York area until 1783; *2nd Bn* served mainly as artillery rather than infantry – in Philadelphia July 1777 to June 1779, New York area until drafted into 1st and 4th Bns in July 1781; *3rd Bn*, New York area until sent to Georgia in 1779, Southern campaign to end of 1782, renumbered 2nd in July 1781; New York area from January 1783; *4th Bn*, New York area until drafted in July 1781 and renumbered 3rd; *5th Bn*, New York area until drafted on April 28, 1778; *6th Bn*, New York area until drafted April 1778. The various battalions were in many actions (see chronology chapter above); last musters in October 1783. *Uniform:* see Plate F.

New York Rangers, 1st Independent Company of Raised in New York in late 1776, under Capt Christopher Benson; part of the NYC garrison until disbanded. *Uniform:* short red coats with blue cuffs and lapels, black hat with black feather.

New York Volunteers First recruits were Loyalist refugees, formed into two companies under Capts Grant and Campbell, who sought protection at Sandy Hook; taken to Halifax and brought back to New York in summer 1776; fought at Long Island "almost naked and extremely feeble from a long series of fatigues" (W.O. Raymond, *Winslow Papers 1776–1826*, St John, 1901: 43). Three companies from April 1777 under LtCol George Turnbull, four companies from April 1778. Sent from New York to South Carolina in December 1779 (storm diverted ship carrying Althaus' company of riflemen – see next entry – to England). Troop of "mounted infantry" under Maj Coffin from September 1780; to New York area in December 1782; last musters October 1783. *Uniform:* red (1777 List). Clothing bills of 1780 and 1781 mention scarlet, blue facing cloth with lace and red, blue and white thread and "trimmings" for sergeant's uniforms, as well as hats, shirts and shoes. Lt Alexander Johnston's uniform was trimmed with silver lace and epaulettes (Public Archives of Nova Scotia, White Coll, Vol.2); "Red Coat, Buff Lappel Variety Trimming" (1783 NY List); red coats faced with blue, no button color indicated for officers (Wiederhold).

New York Volunteer Rifle Company Raised late 1776 as part of Emmerich's Chasseurs; transferred to New York Volunteers, and finally to Queen's Rangers, with which it campaigned in Virginia during 1781 under Capt John Althaus. *Uniform:* green jackets when with Queen's Rangers, according to Simcoe's journal.

North Carolina Highland Regt Following a call to arms on January 10, 1776, loyal Highland settlers assembled at Brunswick, NC, in February and were formed into companies under Governor Josiah Martin. Defeated at Moore's Creek Bridge, NC, on February 27 and dispersed thereafter. When British forces moved into the South during 1780, Gen Cornwallis consented to the Highlanders forming a regiment led by Governor Martin; apparently on pay strength from June 1781, with LtCol Alexander Stewart commanding; had some 40 officers with women, children and slaves, but few enlisted men; formed into two companies by December 1781; reduced to one company of

Col Edmund Fanning, King's American Regiment, c.1780 – a portrait made by Goddard and engraved by B.Reading. The uniform shown in this contemporary engraving would be a scarlet coat with dark blue or green facings, gold buttons and lace. (Library and Archives Canada, C46911)

36 NCOs and privates stationed at Fort Arbuthnot, SC, in 1782 under Capt Neil McArthur "Commanding North Carolina Highlanders." To St Augustine, Florida, and merged into North Carolina Volunteers in 1783. *Uniform:* on February 17, 1776, Governor Martin bought some "plad hose" with shoes and some buttons, thread and cloth and "Silk for a pair of Colours" (AO 13/4). For the 1780 corps: "Blue Jackets are making as fast as possible ... which with the plaid of the 71st will at least keep them comfortable until proper clothing arrives from England ..." – as October 10, 1780 letter to Lord Cornwallis (Haarmann, *JSAHR*, XLIX: 149)

North Carolina Independent Company In pay records June 1781 to October 1783 under Capt Eli Branson. Attached to New York Volunteers in c.August 1783, and dissolved thereafter.

North Carolina Light Dragoons (aka **Wilmington Light Dragoons** and **North Carolina Independent Dragoons**) Raised at Wilmington under Capt Richard Gillies (also named as Gordon, Gilles and Gillis) in June 1781; men all aged 23 or less, and an "exceeding pretty Troop," as the captain "clothed them at his own expense" in July. At John's Island, SC, from fall 1781; Capt Gillies killed in action on August 29, 1782; troop dissolved thereafter.

North Carolina Volunteers (aka **Royal North Carolina Vols** or **Regt**) Raised from February 1779 under LtCol John Hamilton; at Hillsborough and Wilmington, 1781; took casualties at Charleston, and to Quarter House, SC, in 1782; ten companies (257 all ranks) evacuated to St Augustine that November; disbanded in 1783. *Uniform:* see Plate D.

Pennsylvania Loyalists Raised in Philadelphia from October 1777 under LtCol William Allen; was to have three battalions, the 2nd to "consist of the natives of Ireland; and the third of firm and faithful Catholics" (*Scots Magazine*, December 1777); in fact had six companies. To New York area in July 1778; to Pensacola via Jamaica that October; merged temporarily with Maryland Loyalists, December 1779 (see **United Corps of Pennsylvania & Maryland Loyalists**); distinct unit again after Pensacola's surrender to Spanish, May 1781. Sent to New York from Havana, Cuba in July; officially exchanged on July 24, 1782; served in New York area until settled in New Brunswick and disbanded on October 10, 1783. *Uniform:* possibly green coats in 1777–79; red coats with green facings, white lace with a yellow and a green line from the Loyal Irish Regt, issued during its stop in Jamaica in December 1779; "Red Coat – Olive Lappel Variety button hole" (1783 NY List). Red coats faced with green, gold buttons for officers (Wiederhold).

Philadelphia Light Dragoons *1st Troop* raised in Philadelphia from November 1777 under Capt Richard Hoveden; mentioned at review in Philadelphia, May 1778 (Library of Congress, Ms Division, 6B, Vol.2, 1st Bn Brigade of Guards Orderly Book, May 8, 1778); attached to British Legion and Queen's Rangers; incorporated into King's American Dragoons, 1782. Said to have worn green jackets. *2nd Troop* raised in Chester County from January 1778 under Capt Jacob James; mentioned at review in Philadelphia, May 1778. Both troops dissolved from c.July 1778, when British evacuated Philadelphia.

Prince of Wales' American Regt Raised in Connecticut from October 25, 1776, under BrigGen Montfort Browne as colonel; 560 men in ten companies complete by April 1777. Raid on Danbury, CT, on April 27–28; posted to New York and vicinity, January 1778; in Rhode Island, June; in New York from December 1779; to South Carolina, March 1780; siege of Charleston; action at Hanging Rock, August 6, 1780; back in New York, January 1783; to Nova Scotia in September, and to St John, New Brunswick, Canada, for disbandment and settlement (WO 1/13). *Uniform:* see Plate D.

Provincial Light Infantry Temporary battalion existing June 1780–January 1782 under Col Watson and Maj Thomas Barclay, consisting of light companies drawn from 1st, 2nd & 4th New Jersey Volunteers, 3rd Bn De Lancey's Bde, Prince of Wales' American Regt, King's American Regt and Loyal American Regt. Campaigned mainly in South Carolina.

Queen's Own Loyal Virginia Regt Raised from November 1775 at behest of Lord Dunmore, governor of Virginia, under LtCol Jacob Ellegood. Elements defeated at Great Bridge near Norfolk, VA, on December 9, 1775. Lord Dunmore's forces remained in Norfolk area until evacuated to New York up to August 1776; regiment apparently dissolved at that time, its officers and men being taken into other services, some joining Robert Rogers' King's Rangers. Capt John Collett, commissioned on March 9, 1776, raised one company under the regiment's name in New York. He "clothed the whole company from head to foot" at his "considerable expense" since it had no clothing "and the men were distressed"; some of them came "from Virginia with Lord Dunmore, but Captain Collett enlisted them all" in New York. The unit was reported "better clothed and appointed than Provincials in general" when inspected in February 1777 (AO 13/2). Appears to have dissolved thereafter. *Uniform*: not described.

Officer's gilt shoulder belt plate, King's American Regiment, c.1780; private collection. The garter, set against trophies of flags, arms and drums, bears the motto *PRO REGE ET PATRIA* – "For King and Country"; the scroll below bears the regimental title. (Todd Albums, Anne S.K. Brown Military Collection, Brown University, Providence, USA; author's photo)

Queen's Rangers Authorized on August 6, 1776, successively commanded by Robert Rogers, Christopher French (May 1777), James Wemyss (August 1777), and finally John Graves Simcoe (October 1777) – who proved its most talented leader until its disbandment. Lost 20 killed, 28 missing and 8 wounded in its first actions at Bronx River, October 1776 (CO 5/93); original officers mostly cashiered by Gen Howe, March 1777, due to the "infamous conduct of some ... of the officers in plundering and robbing many people" as well as attempting to steal the soldiers' bounty money. The men were totally reorganized under new officers, taking in some officers and men of the Loyal Virginia Regt and Stark's Corps (CO 5/98). Took part in Philadelphia campaign; in action at Brandywine and Germantown in 1777, and Monmouth in 1778. On the American establishment from December 2, 1779, as **1st American Regt.** Sent to Virginia in 1781; took part in Yorktown campaign and defense; most taken prisoner during 1782, the majority interned at Lancaster, PA. Detachments in New York merged into King's American Dragoons that year. On British establishment from December 25, 1782; disbanded October 1783. *Uniform*: see Plate G and illustrations.

Roman Catholic Volunteers Raised in Philadelphia from July 1777 under LtCol Alfred Clifton; had four companies by early 1778. Intended to recruit amongst the "well affected" Roman Catholics who were numerous in Philadelphia, and mainly Irish. Transferred to New York, July 1778. Guarded British army's baggage during defeat at Monmouth but saw no action there. The army's discipline broke down during the retreat to New York; many incidents of plundering and violence to civilians in New Jersey were reported, the Roman Catholic Volunteers being amongst the worst offenders – two captains were later tried by court martial and dismissed. With many of its officers and men compromised, the corps was dissolved in October 1778 and incorporated into other units (CO 5/96).

Royal American Reformees Raised in May 1778 in Bedford, CT, under LtCol Rudolphus Ritzema; nine very weak companies by the summer; no musters after December 1778. Ritzema and several officers shown on half-pay in the 1779 North American Army List.

Royal Foresters Authorized in South Carolina under Capt Andrew Deveaux; failed to attract enough recruits, and dissolved. In early 1783 Capt Deveaux, then a refugee in St Augustine, E.Florida, prepared a daring private expedition to retake the Bahamas from the Spanish – see **Bahamas Loyal Volunteers**, under West Indies.

Royal Garrison Bn – see **Garrison Bn**, under West Indies

Royal Georgia Volunteers Authorized from January 1779 under Maj Dugald Campbell, to

Light infantryman and "huzzar" of the Queen's Rangers, c.1780 – copy of original watercolor by Capt James Murray. Both have all-green jackets; the light infantryman has small white wings to the shoulders, white trousers, short black gaiters, and a black cap with a white crescent badge, a white curved plume and another green-white-green standing plume; the hussar has green trousers, low black boots, a black (fur?) hussar cap with a white crescent badge and a green bag having a white tassel at its end, and a green saddlecloth with white crescents in the four corners. Both have black accoutrements. (Library and Archives Canada)

have infantry and cavalry on the "same footing" as other provincials (PRO, 30/55/9822). Apparently never raised.

Royal North Carolina Volunteers or **Regt** – see **North Carolina Volunteers/Regiment**

Sandford's Troop of Provincial Cavalry Mentioned in Philadelphia in June 1778 as attached to Brigade of Guards Light Infantry (Library of Congress, Ms Division, 1st Bn, Brigade of Guards Orderly Book, May 8, 1778)

South Carolina Light Dragoons Raised from January 1781 under Capt Edward Fenwick; at John's Island, moved to Quarter House, SC, from c.December 1781. Two captains and one trooper killed fighting Marion's Americans on August 29, 1782 (*Royal South Carolina Gazette, September 12, 1782*). Troop dissolved thereafter.

South Carolina Rangers Authorized raised from "Natives of the country ... between the Peedee and Wateree" from June 1780 under Maj Robert Harrison; to have 500 men, but actually recruited only about 100; at Camden until fall of 1781, then to Quarter House. No pay or muster records after December 1781.

South Carolina Royalists Raised from May 1778 under Col Alexander Innis. At Savannah from c.November 1779; at Ninety-Six in summer 1780, Col Innis badly wounded in August; at Camden until fall 1781, then to Quarter House, SC; engaged against Marion's Americans on August 29, 1782; at St Augustine in 1783. Initially an infantry battalion but, from summer 1781, part converted to light cavalry with eight troops (Innis', Frazier's, Archibald Campbell's, Alexander Campbell's, Dawkin's, Kennen's, Harrison's and McLane's) paid as cavalry, and one infantry company (Lindsay's) from that October. Reverted to seven infantry companies (257 all ranks) before evacuation to St Augustine, November 1782 (PRO 30/55/51). Appears to have had many black soldiers in its ranks. White troops to Nova Scotia, and disbanded October 10, 1783; black soldiers to the West Indies, and continued to serve there as **Carolina Corps** – see under West Indies. *Uniform*: see Plate H.

Starckloff's Light Dragoons Organized in Charleston in April 1781 with some 60 Hessian soldiers under Capt Freidrich Starckloff, placed on provincial establishment and served during that year. Seems to have dissolved in 1782. *Uniform*: short green jackets (Haarmann, *JSAHR*, XLIX: 151)

Stark's Corps (aka **New Hampshire Volunteers**) Raised under Maj William Stark from December 1776; four companies authorized, but actual strength barely one. Reported in New York, May 1777; at Philadelphia that December. Probably disbanded during 1778; officers on half-pay in 1779 list.

Stewart's Provincial Light Dragoons (aka **Stewart's Light Dragoons, Stewart's Troop of Guides and Expresses**, and **Staten Island Troop of Light Horse**) Raised and stationed on Staten Island, NY, from 1779 under Capt W. Stewart. Skirmished in New Jersey; amalgamated into King's American Dragoons in 1782. *Uniform*: deserter wearing "scarlet coat, blue facings, buff waistcoat and brown stuff breeches, and boots" (NY *Royal Gazette*, June 15, 1780)

United Corps of Pennsylvania & Maryland Loyalists – see under East and West Florida; also **Pennsylvania Loyalists**, and **Maryland Loyalists**.

Volunteers of New England Raised in New York from April 1781, mustered barely 30 men under LtCol Joshua Upham, down to one sergeant and 24 men at Lloyd's Neck in June 1782; merged into King's American Dragoons.

Volunteers of Ireland Raised in Philadelphia from May 25, 1778, by Col Lord Francis Rawdon, transferred to New York that July. Taken onto American establishment as **2nd American Regt** on May 2, 1779; to Charleston, December 1779, and fought with distinction in the Carolinas; remained in South Carolina until latter part of 1782, then to New York. Taken onto Irish establishment, June 1782, effective from October 1 (CO 5/106). Instructions from London, September 1782, to draft its enlisted men into other British or provincial units and reassign or release its officers (CO 5/55). The officers and NCOs left for Ireland in October. The regiment was on the British establishment as the **105th Foot** from December 25, 1782, but merely to provide half-pay for its officers. *Uniform:* see plate F.

Wentworth's Regt Raised under auspices of Governor Wentworth of New Hampshire, under command of Capt Daniel Murray, from about 1777. On Long Island that October, and remained in New York area; consisted of a single weak company of 25 to 50 all ranks; last pay list in June 1782. *Uniform:* 1777 List mentions red coats for "Governor Wentworth's Volunteers (50 men)."

West Jersey Volunteers Raised in New Jersey from March 1778 under LtCol John Van Dyke; had six companies. Long Island in July; "dissolved and incorporated into other Provincial Corps" that October (CO 5/96). *Uniform:* May have been green (*Pennsylvania Packet*, April 8, 1778).

CANADA

Artificers Formed in Québec City during 1775 by Office of the Board of Ordnance; employed notably at repairing small arms including "old French muskets," making sleighs for field pieces and repairing garrison carriages; served during the siege of Québec. December 1775 had seven armorers, seven carpenters, three smiths, three coopers and three laborers (skilled men), plus 120 artificers. Remained on duty after the siege until fall 1776. A few specialist artisans remained part of Ordnance detachment at Québec thereafter (WO 50/12; *Journal of Thomas Ainslie*), overseeing many artificers – 266 drew rations in Canada in August 1778 (T 64/115). *Uniform:* green coat with scarlet collar, cuffs and lapels, buff waistcoat and breeches.

Batteaumen [*sic*] Company served with Gen Burgoyne's 1777 expedition under Capt Peter Van Alstine; surrendered at Saratoga on October 17; released and dissolved. Another company reported under Capt John Munro, paid September–November 1777 (T 64/115). Another under Capt Jost Harkimer, of three officers, six foremen and c.20–24 workmen, in pay June 1780–April 1782. There may have been other units.

Butler's Rangers Raised among American Loyalist refugees in Canada from September 15, 1777, under Maj (LtCol from 1780) John Butler, with HQ at Niagara. Raised one company at a time during 1777–78 until the corps had eight. The most effective British unit operating out of Canada, it constantly took the war into the heart of enemy territory, as far as New Jersey, Virginia and Kentucky. American historians have often accused the unit of "inhumanity" during its raids; but the Rebels did not endear themselves to the Rangers when the latter learned that captured Loyalist officers had been hanged, while every group of refugees arriving in Canada had new tales of cruelty and outrage at the hands of the enemy. In July and November 1778 the corps raided the Wyoming and Cherry valleys, PA. During 1779 they harassed Gen Sullivan's American force moving through the Iroquois country of northwestern New York. Frontier raids continued into 1780, with one company then based at Detroit, MI; with the King's Royal Regt of New York they defeated a large rebel force on October 19 at Fort Hendrick's Ford. In January

Rifleman of the Queen's Rangers, c.1780, after a James Murray watercolor. All-green jacket with small white wings at the shoulders, white metal buttons; white gaiter-trousers, black half-gaiters; black cap with white crescent badge, white-and-black curved plume and another black-white-black standing plume; black slings for powder horn and, presumably, bullet bag or cartridge pouch. The black stock over the white shirt collar is clearer in this image. (Library and Archives Canada)

Grenadier of the Queen's Rangers, c.1780, after a James Murray watercolor. All-green jacket with larger white-laced wings at the shoulders and buttoned-back "winged" lapels; green waistcoat; white breeches and stockings, black half-gaiters; tall black cap with a white-and-black curved plume and another green-white-green standing plume; black accoutrements. (Library and Archives Canada)

1781 the corps had eight companies and was recruiting another two, the tenth completed by September. From February 1781, with Indian allies, the Rangers blockaded Fort Stanwix, which the Americans abandoned in May; they made more raids that October into the Mohawk Valley, where Walter Butler, John Butler's son, was killed in action at West Canada Creek on October 30. In August 1782 a party of Rangers went as far as Kentucky to raid the fort at Bryant's Station. After the war ended in April 1783 the corps disbanded in June 1784, most of its 469 men, 111 women and 257 children settling in Canada's Niagara peninsula. *Uniform*: see illustrations and Plate C.

Canadian companies The great majority of French-Canadians, then referred to as "Canadians," wished to remain neutral in what they viewed as a war between their former enemies, and they had no wish to serve outside Canada. The 1777 call to form three 100-man companies to join the British army about to march down into New York colony was universally ignored. To encourage enlistment, Governor Carleton announced that two married men would be pressed into service for every unmarried deserter, which considerably upset the Canadian populace. The companies were recruited to strength, but the men's service was uninspired. They were led by Capts David Monin, René Amable Boucher de Boucherville and Hertel de Rouville. Monin's company was from the Montréal, Boucherville's from the Québec and Rouville's from the Trois-Rivières districts. Monin's and Boucherville's went with Burgoyne's army, and Rouville's with St Leger, being employed at the siege of Fort Stanwix. Following Burgoyne's surrender at Saratoga the officers and men of the two companies with his army were released by the Americans, and dismissed on their return to Canada. The enlisted men in Rouville's company were dismissed, the officers kept in service until the end of 1783 (CO 42/46). Numbers of French-Canadians nevertheless continued to be employed by the British army thereafter – probably as "voyageurs" and in other support roles – since some 647 were being "victualled" by the Commissariat in 1778 (T 64/115). *Uniform*: Officers apparently had scarlet coats with dark blue facings, silver buttons and lace; according to Specht's Journal, the men's clothing in 1777 consisted of "brown camisoles and very short jackets, which according to the company were trimmed in red, green or blue ribbons, and of round ungarnished hats trimmed with the same sort of ribbons." It seems that the French-Canadian militiamen did not "choose the [uniform] clothing intended" for them in 1777, but preferred their own style of costume, which was practical on expeditions. They were issued "blankets, kettles, firewood, &c in like manner as the [British and German] Troops" (Add Mss 21,699).

Detroit Volunteers Company of 47 all ranks raised in 1777 at Detroit and in the northwest among fur traders, under Capt Guillaume Lamothe. Reportedly well behaved, they "drilled all winter," with more training in target shooting and entrenching in late April 1778. They garrisoned Fort Vincennes from late 1778 until the fort surrendered on February 25, 1779. Lt Jacob Scheifflin, captured at Fort Vincennes, escaped and arrived safely at New York City in July 1780 (NY *Gazette*, July 17, 1780).

Indian Department The British Indian Department organized in 1755 by Sir William Johnson (1715–74) was the essential instrument of British policy for the wilderness interior of North America. With the support of the Indian nations and working closely with the British army, the department provided invaluable services during the American Revolution. Although not a "military" department as such it was organized along military lines, with officers commissioned by the governor of Canada. Senior command was filled by Superintendent General Sir Guy Johnson (nephew of Sir William) from 1775 to

1782, succeeded by Sir John Johnson (eldest son and heir to Sir William); they were seconded by Superintendent John Campbell and Deputy Superintendent Daniel Claus. Although of lesser importance, there was also a Superintendent of Indian Affairs in the Southern Department, John Stuart (1700–79), who won the cooperation of the Cherokee and Seminole nations. Below these positions came about ten captains – the senior officers in the field serving among the Indian nations – and 15 to 20 lieutenants, mostly in Canada. Nearly all officers were of British or American origin. There was one Indian, the remarkable Mohawk chief Joseph Brant (Thayendanegea), commissioned captain in 1776 and the most influential of the Loyalist Indians. Under these officers were a variable number of translators, often French-Canadians, and a few clerks. The capacity and success of the Indian Dept to mobilize, provide leadership and supplies to Indian nations for action against the Americans during the war was outstanding.

In June 1775, Governor Carleton of Canada assembled an Indian council at Montréal both to secure their alliance for the British and also to impose limits on their raiding in order to prevent acts of barbarity. After a year of this policy, Joseph Brant, speaking for all the warriors, denounced it as an obstacle to the "best method for us to make war in our own way." Brant's view was supported by Lord Germain in London, and the policy was abandoned in late 1776. By then the rebellion had become a full-scale war.

Working closely with Loyalist units, especially Butler's Rangers, the Indian Dept convinced Indian nations – especially the Iroquois – to fight the Americans in earnest, winning a series of victories. Among the main engagements were Oriskany, Wyoming Valley, Cherry Valley, Minisink, Mohawk Valley, Schoharie Valley, the Lochrie expedition, Sandusky and Blue Licks. In return the Iroquois suffered from Gen Sullivan's expedition through their territory in 1779, although the Americans did not dare attack them at Fort Niagara where they had retreated. That fort was the main post for Indian Dept officers, an important supply centre for the Indians, and the usual starting-point for raids into western New York and Pennsylvania.

The end of the war in 1783 was disappointing to many Indians and, like American Loyalists, thousands moved north to resettle in Canada. The Indian Dept continued to be their political and military ally in Canada until 1830, when it was transformed into a civil department. *Uniform*: see Plate C and illustrations.

Col John Graves Simcoe, the talented officer who commanded the Queen's Rangers 1777–83. Dark green coat with dark green collar and black lapels; silver buttons, "teardrop" lace and epaulettes. (Print after J.L. Mosnier; author's photo)

Johnson's Greens – see **King's Royal Regt of New York**

King's Loyal Americans The origin of this corps was a band of about 100 Loyalist refugees from the Albany area who came to Canada in 1776, led by the brothers Ebenezer and Edward Jessup, with the declared intention of fighting for the Crown. Its early formation was informal. and the group was attached to the King's Royal Regt of New York until June 7, 1777, when the King's Loyal Americans was ordered organized under LtCol Ebenezer Jessup. The corps was part of Gen Burgoyne's expedition; following his surrender at Saratoga it was permitted to return to Canada, not being considered a regular unit. Thereafter it was mostly stationed at Pointe-Claire and Lachine, west of Montréal, until September 1778 when its HQ moved to Sorel. It occasionally sent small groups of scouts into northern New York and Vermont; in October 1780 a detachment took part in a raid in upper New York State. It merged with other small Loyalist corps in Canada to form the Loyal Rangers, of seven companies under Maj Edward Jessup, on November 12, 1781. *Uniform*: see Plate E.

Lt Louis de Salaberry, Canadian companies, c.1777–83. He is shown in what appears to have been the uniform for the officers of these companies: scarlet coat with dark blue collar and lapels, silver buttons and silver lace edging; silver epaulettes over scarlet wings edged with silver, both showing blue piping under the lace; and a buff waistcoat. Salaberry was wounded twice at the 1776 siege of St Jean by the Americans. The following year, he took part in St Leger's ill-fated expedition in Capt De Rouville's company. At the end of the war in 1783 he was put on half pay. (Musée national des beaux-arts du Québec; author's photo)

King's Royal Regt of New York In spite of its title this unit was raised in Montréal. In late spring 1776, Sir John Johnson sought refuge in Canada "with about two hundred followers ... from the Province of New York," and informed Governor Sir Guy Carleton that they "would willingly take up arms, if they could get them." Carleton lost no time and, in June, he authorized Sir John to raise a ten-company battalion; a 2nd Bn was raised from July 13, 1780. The 1st Bn reached its established strength in November 1780, but the 2nd never did. The regiment played a distinguished part in keeping the Americans at bay, and participated in several important raids. Some American historians have reported that the vengeful "Johnson's Greens" or "Royal Yorkers" were much feared by, and often inhumane towards, their former countrymen. The 1st Bn was stationed in the Montréal area, the 2nd further west at Oswego and Carleton Island. The regiment was part of St Leger's expedition to Fort Stanwix in 1777. Thereafter detachments were involved in many actions and raids on the New York frontier: punitive raids along the Mohawk and Schoharie rivers in August 1780; a raid on Ballstown on October 16; the defeat of a strong rebel force at Stone Arabia Heights and Hendrick's Ford on October 19. They helped defeat 1,200 rebels at Johnstown on October 25, 1781; were with Butler's Rangers at West Canada Creek on October 30; raided into the Mohawk Valley in July 1782, and repulsed an American attack on Fort Oswego on February 13, 1783. The 1st Bn was disbanded at Montréal on December 24, 1783, the 2nd at Cataraqui (Kingston, Ontario) in June 1784. *Uniform*: see illustrations and Plate C.

King's Rangers (Rogers') Authorized on May 1, 1779, by LtGen Clinton at New York, to have two infantry battalions, commanded by Robert Rogers of "Rogers' Rangers" fame in the French-Indian War. (NB this unit is not to be confused with Thomas Brown's King's or Carolina Rangers – see above.) Rogers sent recruiting officers to Halifax and Québec in the summer (the latter including his younger brother Maj James Rogers), to enlist refugee Loyalists. Robert Rogers arrived at Québec claiming to have enlisted 700 men at Halifax; Governor Haldiman disliked the hard-drinking Rogers and, when he learned that there were only about 40 recruits in Halifax, with unpaid bills, he dismissed him from command. Maj James Rogers was appointed to lead the unit, which mustered three companies in Canada by 1781. Other recruits in New York, sent to Halifax in late 1781, mustered three nominal companies with only 89 men in May 1782; detached to St John's Island, these were disbanded in October 1783. The companies in Canada were never amalgamated into other units, because the corps had originally been authorized under Gen Clinton's American establishment; it only came formally under Governor Haldiman's direct command in January 1783. It was posted at Saint-Jean south of Montréal, and often detached small parties for scouting expeditions into American territory until disbanded from November 24, 1783. 120 officers and men with their families settled near Kingston, Ontario, in March 1784. *Uniform*: for the companies in Canada, initially probably red faced with green; blue faced with white, c.late 1778–80 – e.g. two sergeants' and two privates' suits of "Blue faced white" issued in December 1779 (BL, Add Mss 21849). Green faced with red from c.1781. Unknown for companies elsewhere.

La Mothe's Detroit Volunteers – see **Detroit Volunteers**

Leake's Corps Raised apparently in late 1777 under Capt Robert Leake, and issued old arms without bayonets and bad clothing; posted west of Montréal at Lachine and Sainte-Geneviève in 1779; mustered four officers and 88 men that June (BL, Add Mss 21818). Merged with other small Loyalist corps in Canada to form the Loyal Rangers of seven companies under Maj Edward Jessup on November 12, 1781. *Uniform*: may initially have been red faced with green; probably blue faced with white in late 1778/early 1779, and green faced with red in 1780–81.

Loyal Rangers (Jessup's) Organized on November 12, 1781, when the King's Loyal Americans and several other small units were merged to form this seven-company corps under Maj Edward Jessup. HQ was at Sorel, with detachments at Isle-aux-Noix, Yamaska and Rivière-du-Chîne. It remained on duty longer than other Loyalist units in Canada, and was only disbanded from December 24, 1784, most of its men settling in what is now eastern Ontario. *Uniform*: see Plate E.

McAlpin's Corps – see **Queen's Loyal Rangers**

McKay's Corps Raised in 1777 under Capt Samuel McKay; served with Burgoyne expedition; two officers and 93 men from the Queen's Loyal Rangers joined unit in August 1777 (WO 28/10); following the British surrender at Saratoga the corps was permitted to return to Canada, not being considered a regular unit. Merged into King's Royal Regt of New York, July 1780. *Uniform*: probably red faced with green in 1777, and blue faced with white from c.1779.

Peters' Corps – see **Queen's Loyal Rangers**

Provincial Marine A local government naval force had existed on the St Lawrence and Richelieu rivers, the Great Lakes and other waterways since the French regime in Canada, using small sailing vessels that were usually lightly armed and mainly used for transport and communications. In 1776 some Royal Navy officers and sailors were detached to serve in Canada with the Provincial Marine; on October 11 a flotilla under Capt Pringle, RN, of some 20 gunboats and other small craft partly manned by the Provincial Marine, beat the American boats on Lake Champlain. There was much naval transport activity down lakes Champlain and George for Burgoyne's 1777 expedition. Flotillas were also maintained on the upper St Lawrence River west of Montréal and on the Great Lakes. In 1780 the Provincial Marine had five vessels on Lake Ontario and nine on Lake Erie, mostly schooners and small brigs armed with two to four swivel-guns, except for the brig *General Gage* that had 14x 16-pdrs and up to 30 men on board. Naval activity on Lake Huron was mainly between Michilimackinac and Detroit. From about 1779 there were foraging voyages and patrols into Lake Michigan past Green Bay, WI. At that time a shipyard and naval base was set up at Carleton Island near Kingston on Lake Ontario. The officers and men of the Provincial Marine included a high proportion of French-Canadians, the others being of British and probably Loyalist American origins (Chambers, Ernest J., *The Canadian Marine*, Toronto, 1905). *Uniform*: Governor Carleton permitted commanders of armed vessels "commissioned for the defence of the province in 75 and 76 ... to wear the uniform of lieutenants of the Navy." The use of this uniform by "provincial" officers drew strong protests from Royal Navy officers; Carleton therefore requested that Provincial Marine officers wear "a white button on their blue coat" instead of gold buttons. But the Royal Navy "did not think all this satisfaction enough," even though Provincial Marine officers had often avoided blue coats since the first complaint had been made; an incensed Carleton drew attention to the "zealous and gallant

Sgt Adam Vrooman, Butler's Rangers, with his young son. This image is reproduced from the 1915 *Niagara Historical Society* bulletin No.28; the original painting of c.1785–90 is regrettably now lost. Although unclear, the image shows a dark coat with light-hued collar and lapels, and possibly cuffs, which might confirm the dark green regimentals being faced with red. A sash is worn at the waist, as was proper for a sergeant. The waistcoat appears to be slightly lighter than the lapels, and is probably a creamy buff; what seem to be gaiter-trousers are of the same hue. The headgear is very unclear; it might be a black hat worn fore-and-aft, or a black cap, although the latter seems less likely. The dark leather shoulder belt, perhaps for a hanger, has an oval plate. (Author's photo)

Daniel Claus, Deputy Superintendent of the Indian Department, c.1780. Born in Germany, Claus came to America in 1748 at the age of 21, became an interpreter to the Mohawk Indians, and married Anne, daughter of Indian Department Superintendent Sir William Johnson. He remained loyal to the Crown in 1775, and the Americans seized his property; he fled to Canada and, as one of the Indian Dept's senior officers, led its activities throughout the war. This miniature shows him wearing a red coat with buff facings, silver buttons and lace. (Library and Archives Canada, C19120)

assistance" the Provincial Marine officers had made in "repulsing the King's enemies" in Canada, and was ready to take up the matter with Lord Howe and the Earl of Sandwich had the matter not been dropped. The sailors had "slop clothing" (Add Mss 21699, 21801).

Queen's Loyal Rangers Raised as a battalion from May 1777 under LtCol John Peters. Mustered 262 men during Burgoyne's expedition; heavy losses at Bennington; after surrender at Saratoga it was permitted to return to Canada, not being considered a regular unit. Thereafter at Saint-Jean, moving to Sorel in September 1778; detachment made raids in summer 1778. Corps remained understrength, at one company led by Capt Daniel McAlpin from July 1, 1778, and Maj John Nairne from December 5, 1780. Incorporated into Jessup's Loyal Rangers on November 12, 1781. *Uniform*: see Plate E.

Royal Highland Emigrants Two-battalion regiment authorized from June 12, 1775, to be raised among Highlanders settled in the American colonies, each battalion with an establishment of 610 all ranks in ten companies. The *1st Bn*, under LtCol Allan Maclean, recruited in the Montréal area among veterans of the 78th (Fraser's) Highlanders, disbanded in 1763; taken to Québec city in November, they joined other recruits who had come from Newfoundland, making a total of c.250 men. They formed the bulk of the "regular" troops in the garrison when the Americans invested the city in early December; otherwise there were only a company of the 7th Foot, a detachment of British marines and a few gunners present, the rest of the 1,100 defenders belonging to the city's French-Canadian and British militias. The two-pronged American assault during a snowstorm on the night of December 31 was decisively repulsed; the American commander, Gen Richard Montgomery, was killed, along with hundreds of his men in the assault columns who became casualties or prisoners. The siege lasted until May 6, 1776, when British ships arrived from England, a sortie was made and the Americans withdrew. On June 15, Montréal was liberated without a fight, and the American invasion of Canada came to an end. The battalion was mostly stationed in the Montréal area from summer 1776 until the end of the war. It was posted on the island of Montréal itself in 1776, then south of the St Lawrence, with HQ at Varennes in 1777 until moving to Sorel that August.

The corps escaped Burgoyne's disastrous campaign that year, remaining in Canada as part of the garrison. It provided detachments at Isle-aux-Noix in 1778, and even as far as Fort Michilimackinac (on what is now Mackinac Island, MI), where a captain, a sergeant and 22 men served from fall 1780. By May 1782 the battalion HQ had moved to Batiscan, then back to Montréal by October (LAC, MG23, K1/21). Meanwhile, from December 25, 1778, the regiment was placed on the establishment of the British army and numbered as the **84th Foot**; on May 25, 1779, the establishment of both battalions was optimistically raised to 81 all ranks per company, a strength that was never reached in either battalion; on December 25, 1780, this was more realistically adjusted to 67 all ranks per company (CO 5/170 and 174; WO 7/28). At the end of the war the 1st Bn was transferred to Carleton Island near Kingston, Ontario, to await its disbandment, which was announced in regimental orders of June 4, 1784. (For 2nd Bn see under Nova Scotia.) *Uniform*: see Plates B and D.

NOVA SCOTIA, ISLAND OF ST JOHN & NEWFOUNDLAND

Artificers & Labourers (Newfoundland) Raised in early 1778, employed by Board of Ordnance; about 120 strong including 40 embodied volunteers; appears to have been drafted into the Newfoundland Regt raised in 1780. *Uniform*: "clothed themselves in a uniform dress at their own expense," but no description found (CO 194/34 and 35).

Hierlihy's Corps of Independent Companies Four independent companies in pay April

1777–June 1782 under Maj Timothy Hierlihy; initially posted New York; transferred to Halifax, then to island of St John (present-day Prince Edward Island) in July 1778; five companies, totaling 14 officers and 145 men in March 1780; relieved by detachment of Roger's King's Rangers in 1782; disbanded in Halifax in 1783.

King's Orange Rangers Raised mainly in Orange County under LtCol John Bayard, and posted in New York area from December 1776. Feuds among officers and desertion among men in August 1778 (W.O. Raymond, *Winslow Papers 1776–1826*, St John, 1901: 33); only 159 strong when sent to Halifax in October–November 1778. Detachment to Liverpool, Nova Scotia, in December; detachment to South Carolina, 1779–80; over 200 strong in May 1782; disbanded on October 10, 1783. *Uniform*: green (1777 List); probably red faced with orange, 1780–82; "Red Coat, bright Yellow Lappel white button hole" (1783 NY List); red coats faced with orange, silver buttons for officers (Wiederhold); white waistcoat and breeches, white buttons marked K.O.R. (W.L. Calver and R.P. Bolton, *History Written with Pick and Shovel*, New York, 1950: 131)

King's Rangers (Rogers') – see under Canada

Loyal Nova Scotia Volunteers – see **Nova Scotia Volunteers**

Newfoundland Regt Raised from September 1780 under Maj Robert Pringle, to have 300 men in six companies; number of companies reduced to three, 1781. Remained in garrison at St John's; disbanded October 5, 1783. *Uniform*: blue coat with "red lapels and cuffs – slash pockets – white buttons and button holes by two – and white lining. White waistcoat and breeches. Hat laced with white worsted"; drummers had red coats "with the usual lace on the seams and sleeves" (CO 194/35; WO 7/28); officers, silver buttons.

Nova Scotia Volunteers (aka **Loyal,** or **Royal Nova Scotia Volunteers**) Raised in Nova Scotia from October 1775 under LtCol Francis Legge, also Governor of Nova Scotia. Remained in garrison there, mostly posted in Halifax area; disbanded October 10, 1783. *Uniform*: green coats faced white, white waistcoats and breeches, and hats arrived in Halifax in December 1776 and probably issued early in 1777. Officers also had green coats with white facings trimmed with silver buttons and their hats edged with silver lace. Red coats from c.1779; faced with buff, gold buttons for officers (Wiederhold); "Red Coat – Green Lappel plain" (1783 NY List).

Royal Fencible Americans Raised in Boston and Halifax under LtCol Joseph Gorham from June 1775; recruits in Boston sent to Halifax that

This old colored engraving shows Indian Dept officers or officials and Indians in council, c.1780. The officials wear red coats with yellow/buff facings, white waistcoats, buff breeches and white stockings. (Author's photo)

October; in July 1776, LtCol Gorham with 200 men sent to garrison Fort Cumberland – former French Fort Beauséjour at present-day Aulac, New Brunswick, guarding western access to Nova Scotia, which was rumoured to be a target for the Americans. In early November 1776, Americans and Nova Scotia rebel sympathizers blockaded the fort and captured two boats with 57 all ranks (about a quarter of Gorham's men), then laid siege to the fort. Its garrison consisted of Gorham and 172 all ranks of the Royal Fencible Americans; about 30 loyal local men with their families had also taken refuge in the fort. The Americans had no siege artillery and hoped to induce surrender, but Gorham led a determined resistance. Relief force of Royal Marines and Royal Highland Emigrants from Halifax arrived on November 28, and the next day attacked the rebel camp alongside the garrison; the enemy quickly fled the area. The Royal Fencible Americans remained at Fort Cumberland for the rest of the war; disbanded on October 10, 1783. *Uniform*: see Plate A.

Royal Highland Emigrants *2nd Battalion* (for *1st Bn*, see under Canada.) Raised from June 12, 1775 from Highland veterans settled in colonies; battalion establishment 610 all ranks in ten companies, under Maj John Small, with HQ in Halifax. Part of unit sent to relief of Fort Cumberland, November 1776. In early July 1777 a detachment with some Royal Marines routed an American force at the St John River (now St John, New Brunswick), then rebuilt and garrisoned Fort Howe. Regiment designated **84th Foot**, December 25, 1778. Detachments posted in several localities: in 1779 there were

100 men at Windsor, 50 at Cornwallis, 100 at Annapolis and 120 at the St John River; one company was at Placentia, Newfoundland, 1778–83. Five companies sent to Charleston, SC, in April 1781 were present at Eutaw Springs and other engagements; to New York in April 1782. Unit ordered disbanded in Nova Scotia on October 10, 1783, but actually disbanded only in 1784, most of the men settling in Hants County. *Uniform*: see Plate D.

St John's Island Volunteers On November 17, 1775, two American privateers raided Charlottetown, the capital of St John's (now Prince Edward) Island, which had had no garrison since 1768.

 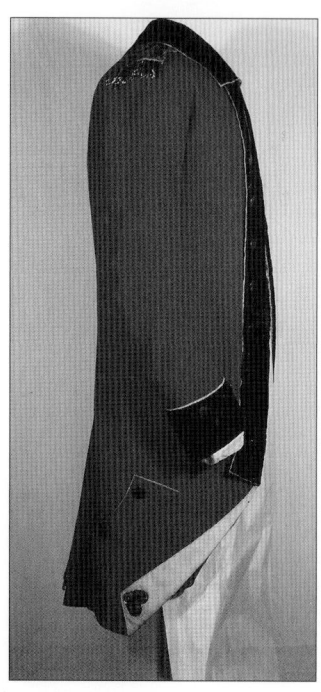

Indian Department coat c.1780, probably worn by Charles-Michel Mouet de Langlade (1729–c.1801). Scarlet with very dark blue collar, cuffs and lapels all edged with narrow white piping; plain silver buttons; shortened skirts, white turnbacks with dark blue heart edged with silver lace; pockets and rear vents piped white. The epaulettes are scarlet shoulder straps piped white, edged with silver lace and garnished with short, thin silver fringes at the end. (Collection & photo: Neville Public Library, Green Bay, Wisconsin)

From March 1776 a provincial company was raised among the loyal men of the island under Capt Philip Calbeck, the administrator of the small colony. Its role was greatly reduced in July 1778 when Hierlihy's Independent Companies joined the garrison, followed by some 200 officers and men of the Hessian Regt von Knyphaussen in October 1779. The corps was to have 100 men, but in December 1779 numbered half that; down to 24 men in May 1782, it was disbanded in October 1783.

EAST & WEST FLORIDA

East Florida Rangers (aka **East Florida Volunteers**) Organized in present-day northeastern Florida and southeastern Georgia from late 1776, under LtCol Thomas Brown; authorized seven white and four black companies, had four troops with only 128 all ranks in January 1777. Took part in frontier campaigns and 1779 defence of Savannah. Incorporated into Georgia Loyalists, June 1782. *Uniform*: linen hunting shirts.

Natchez Volunteers Raised from March 1781 under John Bloomart, as "Corps of Volunteers consisting of eight companies including one of artillery and a troop of horse." Full complement of officers, NCOs and drummers but only 39 infantry privates by June 15, 1781; this increased to 148 by June 24; there were also 19 gunners and 28 cavalrymen, April–June. Took part in siege and recapture of Natchez, April 22–May 4, but mostly dissolved following fall of Pensacola to Spanish on May 10 and recapture of Natchez on June 28. A few officers and men remained on the payroll, apparently at St Augustine, until October 1783 (AO 13/2).

Military Batteaumen Company under Capt Fancis Miller, reported as prisoners of Spanish in Havana, August 1780–June 1782 (PRO 30/55/4951). Possibly taken at Mobile in March 1780.

United Corps of Pennsylvania & Maryland Loyalists Battalion commanded by LtCol William Allen, at Pensacola, from December 1779; had six companies (including a light infantry and an invalid company). Took part in failed relief expedition to Mobile under siege by Spanish, March 1780, and failed assault on Mobile Village on January 7, 1781; at defense of and surrender of Pensacola to Spanish, March 9–10 May; taken prisoner to Havana and repatriated to New York that July. Officers and men officially exchanged –

(continued on page 33)

1: Loyal American Associators, 1775
2: Ethiopian Regiment, 1775
3: Royal Fencible Americans, 1775–76

1: Officer, Québec City Militia, 1775–76
2: 1st Bn, Royal Highland Emigrants; Quebec, 1775–76
3: Loyalist infantryman, Atlantic seaboard provinces, 1776–77

1: Officer, Indian Department, c.1776–83
2: Light Company, King's Royal Regt of New York, c.1776–79
3: Butler's Rangers, c.1778–84

1: 3rd Bn, New Jersey Volunteers, c.1779-83
2: Drummer, 3rd Bn, De Lancey's Bde, c.1781-83
3: Officer, Volunteers of Ireland, c.1779-83

1: Trooper, British Legion, c.1781-83
2: Officer, Queen's Rangers, c.1781-83
3: King's American Dragoons, 1781-83

1: Officer, King's American Regt, c.1780-83
2: Loyal American Rangers (Oddell's), 1781-83
3: South Carolina Royalists/Carolina Corps, c.1782-84

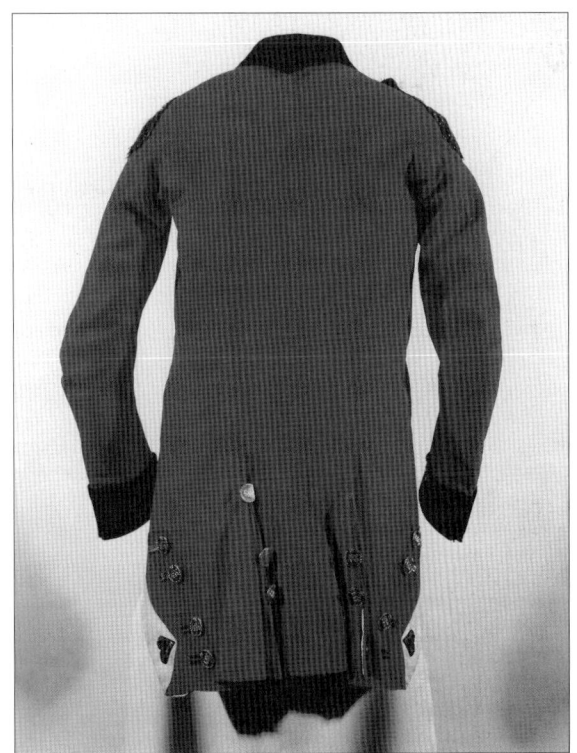

Coatee of Lt Jeremiah French, 2nd Bn, King's Royal Regiment of New York, 1781–84. Scarlet with dark blue collar, cuffs and lapels; gold buttons, lace and "knot" epaulettes; white turnbacks with gold-laced dark blue hearts; white-buff waistcoat. (Canadian War Museum, Ottawa; photo Parks Canada)

i.e. allowed to return to duty – from July 24, 1782. See also **Pennsylvania Loyalists**, and **Maryland Loyalists**, under The 13 Colonies.

West Florida Loyal Refugees Cavalry corps of two companies raised from Loyalists at Pensacola in 1777 under Capt Alexander Cameron and Capt Richard Pearis; employed "in suppressing the rum trade round Mobile Bay" from early 1778 (*American Mss* I:187); third company raised, June 1778, under Capt William McIntosh. Unit seems later to have been reduced to Capt Pearis' company only, which surrendered to Spanish on June 10, 1780.

West Florida Provincial Regt Known to have existed in 1778 under LtCol John McGillivray, from pay lists August–October; had only 67 enlisted men and 17 officers. Took part in "Expedition against the Rebels from Mobile to Natchez, Manchac, and back, between 18th March and 20th November 1778" (T 1/540).

West Florida Royal Foresters Cavalry troop raised from June 1780 under Capt Adam Chrystie; present at failed attack on Mobile Village on January 7, 1781; at defense and surrender of Pensacola to Spanish that May; taken prisoner to Havana and repatriated to New York in July. Only two officers, one sergeant and ten troopers remained; at Long Island until disbanded August 15, 1782.

WEST INDIES & CENTRAL AMERICA

Amherst's Corps Company raised 1780 in New York and Charleston, under Capt Jeffrey Amherst, and sent to Jamaica. There amalgamated into Duke of Cumberland's Regt and Odell's Loyal American Rangers in April 1783.

"Bahamas Loyal Volunteers" Name we arbitrarily give to groups of settlers enlisted initially at Harbour Island (120 men) and Eleuthera (50 men) in early April 1783 by the 24-year-old Capt Andrew Deveaux to join his group of c.70 men drawn from various American Loyalist units at St Augustine. The objective of this private expedition was to retake Nassau, the capital and key to the Bahamas, from the Spanish. Using his commission in the disbanded South Carolina Royal Foresters, Deveaux took command, skilfully landed his force on the island of New Providence on 14 April, and took the weakly garrisoned Fort Montague and a couple of Spanish vessels. More Bahamians joined him, boosting his force to about 500 men. He tricked the Spanish into thinking they faced a much

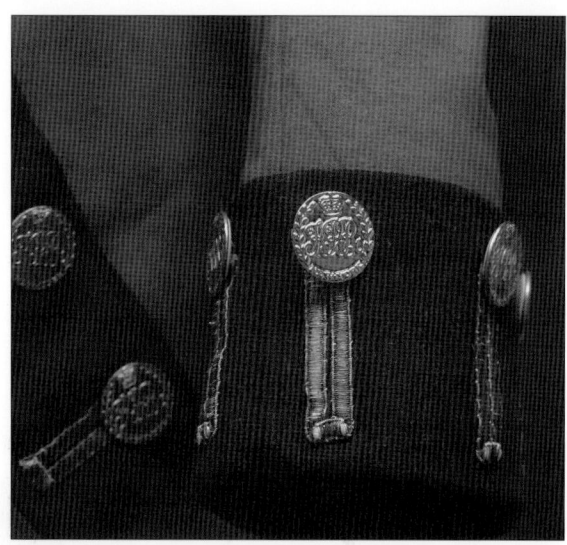

Cuff detail from the coatee of Lt French of the 2nd King's Royal Regiment of New York. The regimental buttons have a central crowned "KRR" in ornate script between side wreaths, and "NEW YORK" below. (Canadian War Museum, Ottawa; author's photo)

larger force than Nassau's garrison of 300 regulars, and he now assumed the rank of colonel — his rank in the South Carolina Militia. His force was joined by most of the New Providence Militia, re-raised after being disbanded by the Spanish. As the Bahamians prepared the heights behind the city for cannon batteries, on April 18 Spanish Governor Claraco capitulated with his garrison, and the Bahamas were once again British – with no casualties incurred on either side. In fairness to the Spanish, they had just been advised that the peace treaty had been signed and had stood down their guards; if Deveaux learned about the peace treaty during the campaign, he rightly chose to ignore it until officially advised. As it turned out, the Bahamas were returned to Britain in the treaty. *Uniform*: none known, but Deveaux was careful to place those of his men who had uniforms – probably red – in prominent view.

Barbadian Rangers Company raised in Barbados under Capt Timothy Thornhill from July 24, 1781, to serve in the Leeward Islands for the duration of the war, and to be sent to St Lucia once completed. In October, Lord Germain wrote from London that once this company had reached 100 men it should be sent to garrison the Dutch colonies of Essequibo and Demerara while further companies were raised. Clothing, arms and accoutrements were to be sent "by the first convoy" for these companies; in the meantime the Rangers would be supplied in the "best manner" possible from resources in Barbados. However, by the end of November the company had only enlisted "more or less 56 men," and local stores lacked the necessary supplies. Gen Christie wished to transfer the company to St Lucia, where provisions could be continued, clothing supplied and more recruits were likely, but this was declined by Capt Thornhill; displeased, the general now doubted the company's use, "at least in this island" (CO 318/7). In March 1782 Gen Christie was advised that necessaries and blankets were being sent to the Leeward Islands for one company of "provincial troops there" – in all likelihood, the Barbadian Rangers (T 27/34).

Carolina Corps In September 1783 a small regular colonial corps of three companies (one of dragoons, one artificers and one pioneers), totaling 326 men led by three white American Loyalist officers, was formed in the West Indies with the refugee African American Loyalist soldiers who had served in South Carolina Loyalist units. This was usually identified as the "Carolina Corps" although it also bore the more official name of **Black Corps of Dragoons, Pioneers and Artificers** on its muster rolls. It served in the eastern Caribbean with HQ in Grenada. (In 1795 the corps was amalgamated to form the 1st West India Regt.) *Uniform*: In 1783, probably that of the South Carolina Loyalists (see Plate H).

Duke of Cumberland's Regt (aka **Montagu's Corps**) Raised from November 1780 in Charleston and Camden under the authority of Governor Dalling of Jamaica, for service in that island, under the command of Lord Charles Montagu; initially five companies of 100 men each, augmented to six companies of 98 all ranks. Many recruits appear to have been soldiers of the American army that had previously surrendered at Charleston. In August 1781 the unit sailed for Jamaica, where it spent the rest of the war, stationed at Rock-Fort near Kingston. A 2nd Bn was authorized in April 1783 by absorbing the Loyal American Rangers. Disbanded in Jamaica on October 24, 1783. *Uniform*: 1781–82, "a short blue jacket with white facings" according to Ebenezer Fox, an American sailor. During 1782 a supply of uniforms for "Provincial Forces in Jamaica" included "Red Light Infantry Coats, Black Facings, White Lace, White Waistcoat & Breeches" with "Light Infantry Hats" for a battalion of 544 privates, almost certainly this unit (T 27/34).

Garrison Battalion (aka **Royal Garrison Bn** or **Regt**, and **Royal Bermudians**) Raised in New York from September 24, 1778, from veterans and invalids unfit for campaign service but equal to garrison duties. Most of the battalion served in Bermuda and the Bahamas; two companies were sent to Bermuda in October 1778, and two others embarked for the Bahamas that November. One company remained in the New York area and furnished a detachment of about 73 men that was present at the unsuccessful defense of Paulus Hook on August 19, 1779; two more companies went to Bermuda that year. The companies in the Bahamas surrendered on May 8, 1782, to a large Spanish force from Havana; they were subsequently exchanged and sent to guard Landsguard Fort, England. The c.75 men at New York were augmented to three companies during 1782. The four companies in Bermuda included a grenadier company; and a fifth company was sent there from New York in January 1783, leaving two companies in New York. The battalion was placed on the British establishment from December 25, 1782. The two companies in New York were disbanded in August 1783, the five companies in Bermuda on about October 5, a company at Halifax on October 10, and the two companies in England probably soon thereafter. *Uniform:* one Robert Dunbar "of the invalids" may have belonged to the unit; he deserted in Philadelphia in September 1780 wearing "a green regimental coat, white jacket and breeches, woollen stockings" (*Pennsylvania Journal*, September 13, 1780); red coats faced with blue, gold buttons for officers (Wiederhold); "Red Coat – Same Lappel Green Cuff & Collar – Variety button hole" (1783 NY List). In April 1781 the battalion commander, LtCol H. Donkin, inquired to Lord Amherst about having distinctive insignia on its "Colours, painting drums, buttons ... being ornamented with a mural Crown" and the motto "CUM MULTIS ALUS &c.," but no reply seems to have been made, and the matter probably went no further (WO 34/174).

Independent Companies (Mosquito Coast) Two companies under Capts Davis and Park formed at Bluefields in present-day Belize in March 1781, from the remnants of several other Jamaican and Mosquito Coast provincial units. They seem later to have been amalgamated into Odell's Loyal American Rangers.

Jamaica Legion Raised in Jamaica in late 1779, "mostly composed of sailors," numbering c.210 men formed into four companies. To Central America, February 1780; took part in capture of Fort San Juan, Nicaragua, April 29; ravaged by fever, remnants incorporated into Jamaica Volunteers on October 29, 1780.

Jamaica Rangers The first "Ranger" unit made up of free blacks and mulattoes who volunteered to serve with regular troops in Jamaica was reported in October 1777 as being raised in and around Kingston. This unit was to act mainly as rangers, but no further information about it appears to be known. In June 1782 royal authority was given to proceed with "raising two Battalions of Free Mulattoes and Blacks" in Jamaica as "a means of removing the [British] Regular Troops to more healthy Stations, by which a number of very valuable lives may be preserved" (CO 137/82). The 1st Bn was led by Maj William Henry Ricketts, the 2nd by Maj William Lewis. A 3rd Bn, authorized on August 14 under Maj Nathaniel Beckford, was also raised and is listed in the 1783 Jamaica Almanack. *Uniform:* 1777, white with red facings; no information on the 1782–83 corps.

Jamaica Volunteers (aka **Royal Jamaica Volunteers**) Raised in Jamaica from October 21, 1779, under Maj J. Macdonald; c.240 men

Front view of Lt French's uniform, showing the scarlet dress waistcoat with gold regimental buttons and laced buttonholes, and the buff-white breeches which also form part of this rare original uniform. (Canadian War Museum, Ottawa; author's photo)

Royal Highland Emigrants camp color, c.1775–83. The field is dark blue, with red crown, cipher, lettering and edges. (Canadian War Museum, Ottawa; author's photo)

formed into five companies. To Central America, February 1780; took part in capture of Fort San Juan, Nicaragua, on April 29; ravaged by fever; March 1781, remnants incorporated into the Independent Companies – see above (CO 137/76–80).

Lewis' Corps of Light Dragoons (aka **Light Horse**) Raised in Jamaica under a Maj Lewis from July 1780; c.98 men, half sent to Central America. March 1781, incorporated into Independent Companies – see above (CO 137/80).

Loyal American Rangers William Odell, "a Major in the Island Militia, an active and spirited young officer" from Jamaica, was sent to New York City in May 1780 to recruit this corps "intended for the Spanish Main," as its "Major-Commandant" (CO 137/77). He recruited many American prisoners of war as well as Loyalist refugees, and arrived in Kingston, Jamaica, with c.300 men in February 1781. The establishment of ten companies each of 50 men was optimistic, and was reduced to six companies each of 77 all ranks. In 1782 a detachment of 80 men under Maj Campbell was part of LtCol Despart's expedition to the Mosquito Coast that recaptured settlements on the Black River from the Spanish in late August. Odell died on January 6, 1783, and his officers and men were thereafter assigned to 2nd Bn, Duke of Cumberland's Regt – see above. *Uniform*: see Plate H.

Mosquito Shore Volunteers (Mosquito Coast) Company of 50 mainly free men raised at Black River in November 1779 by James Lawrie; reported clothed and armed, but had no drums or colors (CO 137/79). Took part in capture of Fort San Juan, April 29, 1780; March 1781, disbanded or drafted into the Independent Companies at Bluefields – see above. Two other units – the Black River Volunteers and Rattan Volunteers, under Capts Richard Hoare and James Ferral – were also in existence from June 1780, but appear to have been militia volunteers rather than provincials, organized for an "expedition on Foot against the Negroes now in Rebellion at Black River Mosquito shore" (CO 137/78).

Royal Batteaux Corps Raised in Jamaica in late 1779; 125 men to Central America in February 1780; at capture of Fort San Juan, April 29; ravaged by fever, and remnants incorporated into Jamaica Volunteers, October 29, 1780.

Turks & Caicos Islands Company In October 1781 clothing was to be sent from London "with all expedition" for a "Company of Soldiers to be raised for the defence of the Turks Islands" in 1782; authorized two sergeants, four corporals, two drummers and 50 privates plus officers. Uncertain if the company ever actually stood guard in the Turks & Caicos; early in 1783 a French squadron from Haiti occupied the islands, which surrendered at discretion since resistance was useless against such a force. (The young Capt Horatio Nelson, RN, attempted unsuccessfully to recapture the main island of Grand Turk on March 9.) *Uniform*: "Short Light Infantry Coat, lined with Osnabrug, 2 Osnabrug Jackets with sleeves & 2 Osnabrug Trowsers, with Leggings to button on the Ancle with Shoes, and Coarse Brown Linen Yarn Stockings, as usual in the Army, with a Hat or Cap" (T 27/34).

Young's Company (Mosquito Coast) This unit, seemingly a pioneer company, is mentioned in a return made at Black River on November 20, 1780, as commanded by Capt Daniel Young. Most of its soldiers were slaves hired from their owners, probably among the 46 or 47 laborers hired in August at Black River and/or Rattan and sent to make repairs at St John's Castle. These men were reportedly "disaffected and averse to the Service" in September; they were probably dispersed following the British evacuation of St John's Castle in January 1781 and the occupation of Black River by the Spanish. (Stephen Kemble Papers, William L. Clements Library)

LOYAL VOLUNTEER MILITIAS

The Loyalists also raised and maintained a substantial number of militia and unpaid volunteer units, especially in cities secured by the British forces. Some major examples were as follows:

Boston

The first large city to be surrounded by the American forces during the summer of 1775 had a strong British garrison, but the city's population was largely in favor of the patriots, so its militia remained inoperative. In the fall, however, a number of men who wished to assist the British forces volunteered their services. These included the **Royal North British Volunteers**, a company of Scots merchants raised in Boston from October 29, 1775, which was "Distinguished by a Blue Bonnet with a St Andrews Cross on it." **The Loyal Irish Volunteers** was a company of "some Irish Merchants" raised in Boston on December 7, who wore a white hat cockade. The **Loyal American Associators** was a unit of three companies organized in Boston on November 17, from men who "offered their service for the defence of the place," and led by BrigGen Timothy Ruggles (see Plate A). These units vanished when the British evacuated Boston in March 1776.

Québec

The first substantial mobilization of loyal militiamen occurred as the result of the American patriots' invasion of Canada in the fall of 1775. Some militiamen were called up in Montréal and its vicinity, but the Americans swept through and reached the outskirts of the fortress city of Québec in November. At the end of that month Governor Carleton called the city's militia into service; it was divided into the "*Milice canadienne*" for the francophone inhabitants, mustering 543 men, and the "British Militia" for anglophone residents, with about 350 men. Some 400 sailors who were in the city were also embodied. The militiamen fought bravely in the repulse of the American assault during the night of December 31. In early March 1776 a militia company of invalids was formed from among those incapable of heavy garrison duties but equal to guarding prisons and stores. The Québec militia were a soldierly-looking body during the siege; in March, Lt Ainslie noted at a parade that the militiamen "had their arms in excellent order and looked very well considering all things" relative to a winter siege. The militia was dismissed in May, except for the battalion of seamen and a volunteer militia company under Capt Beaujeu, who appear to have remained on duty until the fall of 1776. *Uniform*: see Plate B.

Nova Scotia

During 1775 the authorities were increasing worried about unfolding events, fearing that some of the province's population might rebel. In September every regiment of county militia was ordered to organize a "Light Infantry Company" among the "well affected men." At the end of that month some 400 militiamen from Lunenberg and 100 Acadians from Clare and Yarmouth counties were mobilized and called to Halifax to garrison the town until more regular troops arrived during mid-October. Thereafter, the militia mostly watched out for American privateers; in October 1778 some of these raiders took the small town of Liverpool, but men of the Queen's County Militia reoccupied it. *Uniform*: There appear to have been no uniforms issued at large to Nova Scotia militiamen, but the officers and perhaps volunteers may have provided themselves with some military dress. The Queen's County Militia was nicknamed "The Queen's Buffs," possibly referring to a facing color (J.F. More, *History of Queen's County*, 1873).

New York City

The city and its adjacent areas remained under British control during the whole war and was the HQ for the Crown forces in the 13 Colonies. The city's population appears to have included a substantial number of loyal citizens, numbers of whom served in the various militia units. In 1777 the volunteers included the **New York Rangers**, *New York German Company* and the **Royal Bergen Volunteers**. Three years later the city's auxiliary forces had over 4,300 men divided into two groups: the City Militia, mustering 40 companies, and the 12 Associated Companies, some of which were uniformed (CO 5/182). In February 1780 the latter consisted of the **Ordnance Loyal Volunteers** (four companies, one uniformed), the **Engineer Volunteers** (one uniformed company), the Quarter Master General's Volunteers (one company), the Loyal Commissary Volunteers (two uniformed companies), the **Barrack Master General's Volunteers** (one company), the **King's Dock Yard Volunteers** (three companies), the **Marine Artillery** (one uniformed company), the **New York Rangers** (one uniformed company), the **Highland Volunteers** (one uniformed company) and the **New York Volunteers** (seven uniformed companies; presented with a pair of colors on July 2, 1781). By October 1782 loyalist sentiment may have been decreasing in New York City; the auxiliary forces now mustered fewer than 3,000 men, most belonging to the four battalions of the City Militia. Of the Associated Volunteer companies, the Highland, Commissariat, Ranger, Marine Artillery and NY Volunteers were still in being, with the new **Massachusetts Volunteer Company**, but

Charles Tarrieu de La Naudière, an officer of the Québec Militia and *aide de camp* to the governor, Sir Guy Carleton, 1775–76. He appears to be wearing the 1775–76 coat of the Québec City Militia: all dark green with silver buttons, and no visible epaulettes. The shoulder belt and gloves are brown leather. (Château de Ramezay Museum, Montréal ; author's photo)

the others had disbanded (PRO 30/55/5792). All these city units had vanished by November 25, 1783, when the British evacuated New York.

The **counties bordering New York City** also had substantial numbers of Loyalists organized into volunteer and militia units. Some, notably the **Loyal Westchester Volunteers** under Col Isaac Hatfield, were involved in many skirmishes with American forces. There were also the **Loyal Queen's County Militia**, the **Loyal King's County Militia** and the **Loyal Suffolk Militia**. The **Loyal Refugee Volunteers** was a corps of three companies reported at Smith Town, Long Island, led by Col Cuyler in 1780 (NY *Royal Gazette*, 31 January 1781). Some of these units were uniformed – or at least their officers were. On February 7, 1780, the officers of the Loyal Queen's County Militia were ordered to provide themselves with a scarlet uniform "faced with blue, with white lining, white waistcoat and breeches, and silver buttons, with a silver epaulet, a well cocked hat with silver button and loops and silver hat bands."

The Carolinas

In the South substantial elements of the population were loyal to the Crown. After the British forces arrived in force during 1780, the loyal inhabitants of Charleston, SC, requested permission to "embody, arm and uniform themselves" into militia companies on August 13 (*South Carolina and American General Gazette*, Charleston, August 23, 1780). They mustered some 400 men divided into 11 companies of militia under Col Richard King; four companies reviewed on January 4, 1782, had a highly satisfying military appearance (*Royal Gazette*, Charleston, January 5, 1782). Other militia units were also raised at Camden and in North Carolina, some taking part in the battle of Camden in August 1780. *Uniform*: the **Charleston Loyal Militia** was dressed "in scarlet faced with blue" (Walter Clark, ed., *The State Record of North Carolina*, XIV: 748). In September 1780, Camden's garrison consisted of "about 500 Tories who all wear red tags in their hats for distinction" (*Maryland Gazette*, October 13, 1780). The **North Carolina Militia** was shown in red faced with white on a map of the battle of Camden.

AFTERMATH

The end of the American Revolutionary War, and Great Britain's recognition of the United States as a nation, was a cruel blow to the tens of thousands of Loyalists, most of whom were still resident in the new country. Given the bitterness that had marked what had been for them a civil war, the "Loyal Americans" could not remain in the new republic. By early 1783 most had lost their property to "patriotic" Americans; many were persecuted and banished from their towns and villages, some had been murdered, and all felt threatened. Although temporarily safe in New York, where most had sought refuge, all knew that exile from their native land was unavoidable.

Placed in a very difficult situation, the British government did all it could to prevent a human tragedy of monumental proportions. Even before the peace treaty was signed the authorities were looking for ways to resettle the Loyalists elsewhere in lands that still flew the Union flag, and the obvious choice was the vast expanse of present-day Canada. Between April and November 1783 five great fleets laden with Loyalist men, women and children successively sailed north. It is estimated that some 20,000 landed and settled in Nova Scotia; another 15,000 arrived on the shores of what would become in 1784 the province of New Brunswick, and a few hundred went to Prince Edward Island. The transfer was largely carried out as a military operation except that, in this instance, officers and men were accompanied by their families and friends, with all the goods that they could bring. The Loyalist provincial regiments from New York were transferred as units to the new land that they would settle; only when on the spot and when the land had been distributed would they formally disband. Thus, the official date for disbandment of many of these units was in October 1783, when all had arrived and were working to erect shelters for the coming winter. It was sensibly believed that men who had been brothers-in-arms should remain together as neighbours in the difficult transition that they now faced.

In central Canada, about 2,000 settled in the province of Québec, many of them southeast of Montréal in the "Eastern Townships." Nearly 6,000 came up by land through the Niagara peninsula or from Montréal to settle in what became Ontario, now Canada's largest province. There too the settlement was largely along military lines. The refugees were not all white Anglo-Saxons, however. Loyalist African American groups settled in Nova Scotia as free people, while others continued to serve as soldiers in the eastern Caribbean. The Iroquois Indians of New York State had largely remained loyal, and consequently had to leave their ancient domain; Joseph Brant led an estimated 2,000 of them to settle on the shores of the Grand River, Ontario.

A glimpse of what many felt in their hearts was represented by one Loyalist woman who, although she had not shed a tear during the war, was overcome with grief while holding her infant child as she watched the transport ships that had brought them sail away from St John, New Brunswick. But loyal they remained, as dour memories were replaced by new challenges and, within a generation, the new communities that they created were thriving. Indeed, although the fact is largely unappreciated in present-day Canada, it was the Loyalists who brought north many of the basic political and cultural institutions that now largely define the modern nation. Like the French-Canadians they joined in their new country, the Loyalists surmounted the consequences of a lost war, and built a new and forward-looking society that preserved their ideals.

Private of the Garrison Battalion, c.1782–83. Made up of Loyalist veterans and invalids unfit for service on campaign, but equal to garrison duties, this unit was posted mostly in the Bahamas and Bermuda; two of its companies were captured when the Spanish took Nassau in the Bahamas in May 1782. This watercolor reconstruction by Derek FitzJames follows the notes in the 1783 New York List: red coat with red lapels, green collar and cuffs, "Variety button hole," white turnbacks, waistcoat and breeches. (Anne S.K. Brown Military Collection, Brown University, Providence, USA; author's photo)

SELECT BIBLIOGRAPHY

Most of the data in this book are taken from primary source documents found mostly in the archives and libraries of the United Kingdom and Canada; see Author's Note on the imprint page at the beginning of this book. The large collection of muster rolls, pay lists and related documents pertaining to American Loyalist corps preserved at Library and Archives Canada (LAC) in Ottawa has been consulted extensively for the unit histories, but for space reasons it is impractical to cite them individually here. Some of the period newspapers consulted are cited in the text.

Allen, Robert S., ed., *The Loyal Americans* (Ottawa, 1983). Catalogue, with good essays, of an excellent but little-known exhibition at the Canadian War Museum and the New Brunswick Museum.

Clark, Walter, ed., *The State Record of North Carolina*, XIV (Winston, 1896)

Cruikshank, Ernest A., *The Story of Butler's Rangers* (Welland, 1893). Still the standard history.

Cruikshank, Ernest A., "The King's Royal Regiment of New York," in *Ontario Historical Society Papers and Records*, XXVI (1931). Excellent source, reprinted as a book with added index, appendices and muster roll by Gavin Watts (Toronto, 1984).

Fortescue, John W., *A History of the British Army*, Vol.3 (London, 1902)

Kochan, James L., *Don Troiani's Soldiers of the American Revolution* (Mechanicsburg, 2007)

Haarmann, Albert W., "Some notes on American provincial uniforms," in *Journal of the Society for Army Historical Research* (cited in text as *JSAHR*, 1971). The essential study on this topic; notably, it reproduces the 1777

This watercolor of the "Encampment of the Loyalists at Johnstown, a New Settlement …" made on June 6, 1784 by James Peachy, symbolizes the fate of more than 40,000 Loyalist Americans who fled the United States after the war. Most soldiers of disbanded units took their families to Canada, like these men from the King's Royal Regiment of New York, who created in the wilderness what later became the city of Cornwall in the eastern part of the present-day province of Ontario. The small figures are shown wearing red coats with blue facings, red or blue waistcoats and jackets, and wide-brimmed round hats; one at left foreground, apparently an officer, has black plumes on his hat. (Library and Archives Canada, C2001)

List, Wiederhold's 1783 Ms Almanack, and the uniform notes in the copy preserved by the New York Historical Society of the 1783 North American Army List. "The roman catholic Volunteers" and "Jamaican volunteer corps" by the same author are covered in the same volume, and "Jamaican provincial corps" in *JSAHR*, 1970.

Lefferts, Charles M., *Uniforms of the American, British, French, and German Armies in the War of the American Revolution 1775–1783* (New York, 1926). A pioneering work; however, the section on Loyalist units should be used with much caution, since some interpretations are now known to have been in error – specifically, erroneous blue instead of black facings for the Queen's Rangers; white facings on the green uniform instead of red for the King's Royal Regt of New York; dubious brass cap plate for Butler's Rangers; green uniforms faced blue instead of grey uniforms for Emmerich's Chasseurs, etc.

Lewis, James A., *The Final Campaign of the American Revolution: Rise and Fall of the Spanish Bahamas* (University of South Carolina, 1991)

Marley, David F., *Wars of the Americas* (Santa Barbara, 1998). Contains much data taken from the fine studies on Loyalist units published since the 1950s in the *Military Collector & Historian* (cited as *MC&H*), the Journal of the Company of Military Historians, and also its series of *Military Uniforms in America (MUIA)* color plates. Index on line at: www.military-historians.org.

An excellent website is also maintained by Mrs Nan Cole and Mr Todd Braisted – The On-Line Institute for Advanced Loyalist Studies at: www.royalprovincial.com.

Loyalist settlers drawing lots for their land, 1783–84, in a print after C.W. Jefferys. The leader of the new settlement, nearly always an officer, wrote the numbers of the plots to be granted on pieces of paper. As the men drew the slips from a hat the land agent wrote the name of each settler on the plot he had picked out, and registered the name and number in his notebook. In some instances the settlers camped in tents until a government agent arrived to assign the land. The British government provided building tools, clothing, seed, livestock and food until the settlers were self-sufficient. (Private collection; author's photo)

PLATE COMMENTARIES

UNIFORMS

Clothing the American provincial corps did not become a priority for the British authorities until 1776, when they took the decision to embody as many Loyalists as possible. Clothing and cloth sent to Canada in 1775 had been intended to satisfy an over-ambitious scheme to mobilize thousands of Canadian militiamen as light infantry. These uniforms – consisting of green coats with scarlet facings, buff waistcoats and breeches – were distributed to the militia and volunteers defending Québec City, and to the first provincial corps raised in Canada.

The American command

While some groups made up of "Loyalists and refugees" may have had green uniforms in Boston as early as August 1775 (according to Joseph Reed), the large-scale outfitting of Loyalist corps in the Atlantic seaboard colonies only got under way a year later. By the fall of 1776, some 5,000 green uniforms faced with white and 5,000 round hats were shipped to New York (see Plate B). Thus it seemed that the "provincials" would all be dressed in green; but there must have been second thoughts about this. In February and March 1777, 3,000 uniforms were shipped to New York consisting of red coats faced with blue, green or white, with white lining, buttons, loops and lace, white breeches and waistcoats (PRO 30/55/356; T 64/106). That some corps were issued red coats during 1777 is reflected in a list of Loyalist units, complete with the coat colors of many of the corps, which was compiled late that year and published early in 1778 in several papers in Great Britain (*Cumberland Chronicle and Whitehaven Public Advertiser*, February 14, 1778; *Scots Magazine*, February 1778) and even in French in the *Québec Gazette* of November 12, 1778. (Note that we refer to this document as the "1777 List" in the Unit Histories above.)

It is clear that by 1778 green coats were no longer in favor except for light infantry and some cavalry units, and otherwise were being replaced with red. In that year mittens, shoes, leggings, white worsted stockings, linen for making shirts, blankets, haversacks, canteens, hand hatchets and other camp items were also sent for the estimated 10,000 provincials in New York, Rhode Island and Nova Scotia (CO /170).

In 1780, this shipment was repeated in most particulars for 10,000 "provincials in Georgia and New York," and 10,000 pairs of "woollen or linen trousers supposed equal to 10,000 pairs of leggings" were added at the suggestion of Lord Amherst, then commander-in-chief of the army (CO 5/174).

In May 1780, a list of 5,575 uniforms shipped mentioned red coats for all (except for 61 drummers); of these 1,167 were faced with blue, 1,167 with green, 1,060 with buff, 1,060 with white, 530 with orange and 530 with black; they were accompanied by waistcoats and breeches of white, or buff for buff-faced units (PRO 30/55/9864).

In 1781 another shipment consisted of 6,405 coats, all red except for 105 drummers' coats, with the same proportion of facings, and with white or buff waistcoats and breeches (PRO 30/55/9904). That same year a shipment to Charleston is listed for Loyalist units, apparently light cavalry: 326 green jackets, 274 drill jackets, and 32 red jackets for militia, as well as cloth. In 1782, clothing and equipment for 500 light dragoons were sent to the South, and more uniforms went to New York (PRO 30/55/10280, 4306).

In no case did the shipments mentioned above identify the corps for which the clothing was intended. However, from 1780 some of the major units were identified in lists of clothing sent to the stores in New York. These corps were the British Legion, the Queen's Rangers, the New York Volunteers and the Volunteers of Ireland (see under Unit Histories, above). Other parts of these lists have only coat and facing colors, not attributed to any unit, but one suspects that at least some of the red coats faced with orange went to the King's Orange Rangers.

More specific attribution of this clothing to units can be attempted with the help of the two manuscript compilations already mentioned briefly under Unit Histories: both were made in 1783 and are now in the collections of the New York Historical Society. Bernard de Weiderhold, a German officer serving with the British army in New York, mentioned the uniforms of many units in his manuscript almanac; while an unknown hand inscribed the uniforms of most corps included in a copy of the list published in New York during 1783. These two lists are often in contradiction as to facings, but they are the most important sources presently known as to the dress of Loyalist units in the 13 colonies and Nova Scotia. Again, they are cited here as "Wiederhold" and "1783 NY List" respectively.

The Canadian command

As mentioned above, Loyalist units raised in Canada were initially uniformed in green faced with red, with buff waistcoats and breeches, in 1775 and 1776. These were the 1st Bn, Royal Highland Emigrants, and the King's Royal Regt of New York (see Plates B and C). In 1777 the Royal Highland Emigrants assumed their Highland dress; red faced with green was issued to the small new Loyalist corps, except for Butler's Rangers, which had green. According to several sources, the British troops of Burgoyne's expedition dressed as light infantry. Thomas Anburey's *Travels through the Interior Parts of North America* explains the situation in a letter written in Montréal on April 6, 1777: The clothing for the army not being sent out [to Canada] last year [1776] and as it will be too late to fit it to the men when it arrives, the commanding officers of the different regiments have received orders to reduce the men's coats into jackets, and their hats into caps, as it will be the means of repairing their present clothing, and be more convenient for wood service, that when the army takes the field, they will in a

A crowned "RP" enlisted man's pewter button, common to most American Loyalist units in 1776–83; the letters stood for "Royal Provincials." Diameter, 22.4mm. Found by archaeologists at Fort Beauséjour National Historic Site (Fort Cumberland), Aulac, New Brunswick. (Parks Canada, RA 151)

41

manner be all light infantry. The regiments have the hair that is fixed to their caps of different colours; ours [Anburey's regiment was the 29th Foot] is red.

This order was probably followed by Loyalist units with Burgoyne's main body of troops going down Lake Champlain, and also by St Clair's troops on the Mohawk River.

In 1778 mittens, shoes, leggings, white worsted stockings, linen for making shirts, blankets, haversacks, canteens, hand hatchets and other camp items were sent for the estimated 2,000 provincials in Canada (CO 5/170). According to Canadian stores records (Add Mss 21,849), the uniforms for provincial corps were either red faced with green or green faced with red, lined white, with white waistcoats and breeches. Officers had uniforms of finer material, with silver epaulettes, silver lace for their hats and "narrow lace for coats," and gross lots of "Officers Silver Plated Coat Buttons" were mentioned. These stores also contained a great many other items such as mittens, "Canadian" caps, stockings, shoes, leggings, "trimmings" for the leggings, "Indian" shoes, "Mogasons" and "Blanket Coats long and short."

There are two recorded deviations from the above. Firstly, by late 1778 the small Loyalist corps in Canada had received blue coats faced with white. The "Officers of the Loyalists" protested to Governor Haldiman on December 2, 1778

> that the Cloathing ... being Blue faced with White, the same as the Uniform of many Regiments of our Enemies, we are apprehensive that should we be sent on service with this Cloathing, many fatal accidents might happen, from mistakes of Indians and our own Scouting Parties, as was actually the case several times last Campaign. We are aware that to expect this Cloathing should be totally laid aside, for such reasons, after the great expense the Crown has been at, must be deemed unreasonable; our wishes only are that Your Excellency will Order us, Red Clothing, as along as any remains in Store, and that the Blue may be made use of the last (Add Mss 21,821).

Secondly, in about 1779 the green coats of the King's Royal Regt of New York were changed for red faced with blue, the uniform it kept until the end of the war. There may have been "a Blue Worm in the men's lace" from 1781 (Add Mss 24,323). All other Loyalist units had become Rangers, and had green faced with red (see Plate E) from about 1780. In the last years of the war brown suits for scouts were also held in the stores. As in the seaboard colonies, records of clothing sent to Canada were not identified to specific units, so that attribution must be uncertain in some cases.

A1: Loyal American Associators, 1775
The most basic costume of all: this three-company volunteer militia unit, organized under Timothy Ruggles in Boston in late November 1775, were issued arms but wore their own civilian clothing, distinguished only by a white "sash" tied around the left arm (WO 55/677).

A2: Ethiopian Regiment, 1775
An account of December 1775 mentioned that the men of Lord Dunmore's "black regiment" had the slogan "Liberty to Slaves" as an "inscription on their breasts" – or rather, on the breast of the clothing they wore. Since they were armed and equipped from British ships lying off Norfolk, VA, it is believed that the men of the regiment generally wore sailors' smock-like "slop" shirts of linen or old sailcloth with the slogan written on the chest. A red ribbon may have also been worn around the crown of their hats. The arms would have consisted of Sea Service muskets for those who were trained to handle firearms, and of boarding pikes and sabers for the others. (Peter F. Copeland, "Lord Dunmore's Ethiopian Regiment," *MC&H*, Vol 58, No.4, 2006)

A3: Royal Fencible Americans, 1775–76
This unit had no regimental uniforms for over a year after it was authorized to be raised. During the siege of Fort Cumberland in November 1776 warm clothing was scarce,

Enlisted man's pewter button of the Royal Fencible Americans regiment, c.1778–83. This button, of 16mm diameter, was also found on the fort site at Aulac, New Brunswick (Parks Canada, RA 151). The drawing reconstructing the design is by Derek FitzJames. (Private collection; author's photo)

and the soldiers were "permitted to wear the Barrack Ruggs and Blanketts" or they would have "otherwise suffer greatly if not entirely perish" of exposure to the cold (Gorham's *Journal*). Green coats faced with white, together with white waistcoats and breeches, and hats, arrived in Halifax in December 1776 and were issued to the Royal Fencible Americans, probably in early 1777. The officers had silver buttons and hats edged with silver lace. The uniform color later changed, and was described as "Red Coat, Black Lappel, White button hole" (1783 NY List).

B1: Officer, Québec City Militia, 1775–76

According to the order books, the uniform specified for all the city's militia companies on November 24, 1775, was "a plain green coat, with buff waistcoat and breeches ... green cloth sufficient to make cuffs and collars"; and on December 12 silver epaulettes were mentioned for officers. So far as is known there was no facing color until the latter part of 1776; but some officers, whose green coats had "straw coloured [buff] facings," were seen by a German officer at the New Year's Eve festivities on December 31, 1776. The seamen embodied during the siege were also dressed "in green, with scarlet facings, cape [collar] and cuffs," according to the recollections of Lt William Lindsay of the Québec British Militia. After the siege was raised in May, Governor Carleton asked the city's militiamen "by no means to take off the cockade from our hats, that being a mark of distinction conferred upon us for our brave behaviour during the siege" (*Scots Magazine*, July 1776, p.361). After the siege, Capt Beaujeu's company of Canadian militia volunteers and the battalion of seamen remained in service; the uniforms they were issued in August were probably green with scarlet facings, with buff waistcoat and breeches (WO 1/11).

B2: 1st Battalion, Royal Highland Emigrants; Québec, 1775–76

Although the regiment was "to be Cloathed, Armed and Accoutred in like manner, with His Majesty's Royal Highland Regiment" (the 42nd or Black Watch), there is no evidence of red uniforms faced with blue or Government tartan plaids being sent and issued to the 1st Bn at Québec (and later Montréal) in 1776. Instead, the recruits arriving at Québec in November and December were issued green coats with red collar, cuffs and lapels, buff waistcoats and breeches. The officers and men had laced hats, the former with silver. Another issue took place in August 1776 and appears to have been generally similar to the 1775 uniform, but included "yards of green cloth for leggings." The men were further instructed on September 1, 1776, to keep their old (1775 issue) uniforms for fatigues (WO 1/11; LAC, MG23, K1/21).

Drawing of a silver belt plate of the Royal Fencible Americans regiment; it bears the name of its owner, Lt Richard Wilson, around the crossed sword and olive branch badge, above PRO REGE ET LEGE – "For King and Law." (*JSAHR*; author's photo)

B3: Loyalist infantryman, Atlantic seaboard provinces, 1776–77

Following the British occupation of New York and the launching of the recruiting drive to raise Loyalist corps, uniforms were ordered to be sent from Britain to America on August 30, 1776 (T 64/106). These were some "5,000 Uniform Suits including 4 Sergeants and 2 Drums to every 100. The Coats green, lined with white Baize, Waistcoat & Breeches white & white Buttons. Cloth & making the same as for the Army and not better," with "5,000 round hats, 5,000 pair of Breeches"; and 10,000 each of pairs of shoes, pairs of stockings, rollers and shirts, and 10,000 yards of woollen cloth for leggings. A thousand uniforms described as "green turned up with white and white waistcoats and breeches" were also received in Halifax, Nova Scotia, by November 11 (LAC, MG 11, NS/A/96). The clothing appears to have been distributed soon after its arrival. The *New York Gazette* mentioned on April 14, 1777, that the corps already raised were "mostly cloathed" and made a "very handsome appearance," reporting their uniform as "chiefly Green, faced with White, and made of the best Materials." The officers had the same uniforms, "but quite plain." This clothing was not distributed in Canada but issued to units serving in the Atlantic seaboard provinces.

C1: Officer, Indian Department, c.1776–83

There appear to have been no formal regulations for Indian Dept uniforms until 1823, before which the informal practice was to wear a scarlet coat. This was initially completely scarlet, and is shown in Benjamin West's well-known portrait of Sir Guy Johnson in 1774 as having silver buttons but no lace, and worn with a buff waistcoat and breeches. At that period the addition of a facing color to the coat collar, lapels and cuffs came into fashion; the portrait miniature of Daniel Claus shows the color as buff with silver buttonhole lace. Langlade's coat (see page 24) has dark blue facings edged with narrow white piping, silver buttons and epaulettes, and no laced buttonholes; but buff seems to have been the predominant facing color used until the 19th century.

C2: Light Company, King's Royal Regiment of New York, c.1776–79

The uniform of this unit was initially green – hence its nickname of "Johnson's Greens" – and probably with red facings, apparently sent from Québec in August 1776. That clothing delivery included green, scarlet and buff material, and laced hats (War Office 1/11). In about 1777 the uniform – as shown here – was described as "a green coat with red facings, and a cap with a lock of red" (Jeptha Simms, *Frontiersmen of New York*, Albany, 1883). The caps may have been only for the light company, since the regimental orderly book also mentions that the men's "Regt'l hats [should be] well Cocked, & their hair Properly Dressed" in May 1777. The regiment was reportedly still wearing green in November 1778, but the next clothing issued was red faced with blue, probably in wear from July 1779. The men's red coats had white

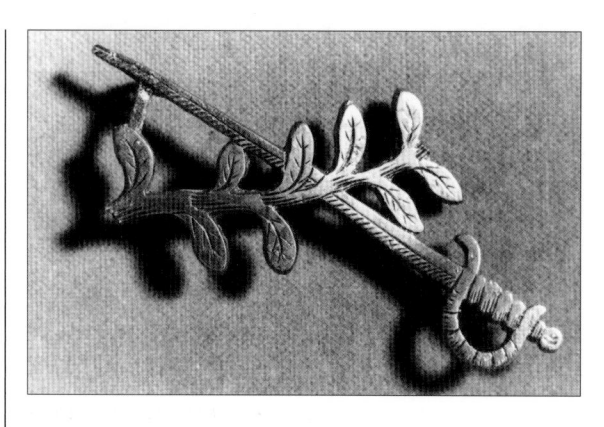

Enlisted man's brass cartridge box badge, Royal Fencible Americans regiment, c.1778–83; found by archaeologists at Fort Beauséjour National Historic Site (Fort Cumberland), Aulac, New Brunswick. (Parks Canada, RA 129)

buttonhole lace, possibly with a blue line. Officers' buttons and lace on the green coats are unknown but were probably silver; this changed to gold in 1779–80 when scarlet was taken into wear, as officers's silver belt-plates were gilded in 1780 (Add Mss 24,323).

C3: Butler's Rangers, c.1778–84

The dress of this unit has been shrouded in some mystery, but it seems to have had green coats from the outset. The uniform worn at Fort Niagara in December 1778 was described in Ernest Cruikshank's history of the corps as being of "dark green cloth, trimmed with scarlet... with a low, flat cap, having a brass plate in front bearing the monogram "G.R." encircled by the words "Butler's Rangers." The source for this description has not yet been found, but Cruikshank – who went on to become one of Canada's leading archivists and historians – was not prone to inventions. Charles Lefferts interpreted the cap device as a brass plate, but it was more likely a transposed cartridge box plate. In any event, the headdress seems to have varied. William Caldwell wore a headscarf instead of his "military hat" when raiding the Wyoming Valley in July 1778, and Walter Butler was said to have worn a gold-laced hat during his last raid in the Mohawk Valley in October 1781. Thus hats may have been issued, but these could easily be made into caps, which were certainly handier for Rangers in the wilderness. Among the "list of sundry articles wanted" by the corps in September 1779 were "2 pieces fine Green cloth for Officers, 4 do white do, 3 do middling Green do for Serjeants, Buttons & Trimmings suitable for the above, 360 Suits of Cloathing for Men, 360 Blanket Coats or Blankets in proportion, 50 pieces of binding for ditto, 1500 pairs men's strong shoes, 1500 shirts, 1440 pairs stockings ... 30 dozen Hats, 40 pieces of

Brass shoulder belt plate, Butler's Rangers, c.1778–1783. (Parks Canada)

Russia Sheeting for Trowsers ... 10 pieces Russia Drilling for Knapsacks," and 360 tin canteens (Add Mss 21,760). Note that there is no mention of scarlet cloth for the officers and sergeants, just as no white cloth is mentioned for sergeants, but these may already have been on hand – this list asks for certain items that were needed, not a whole issue. The clothing for provincial corps listed in Canadian stores featured coats of green faced with red, or vice versa, but no green coats faced with white. An old photo of a now lost portrait of Sergeant Vrooman appears to show lapels that could be red (see page 21). Thus, such evidence as is presently available seems to point to red facings.

D1: Officer, Prince of Wales' American Regiment, c.1777–83

This may have been one of the first Loyalist units to receive red coats rather than green; red is mentioned as its uniform color as early as 1777–78. The blue facings are mentioned in December 1780, when a runaway slave from Capt John Collet's company took "2 green coats turned up with blue, yellow buttons and a gold epaulette" (*South Carolina Gazette*, December 1780) – so the unit may also have had green coats. By the last year of the war Wiederhold's 1783 Ms Almanack listed its uniform as being red coats faced with green, with gold buttons for officers. However, the notes in the 1783 New York North American Army List read: "Red Coat – Blue Lappels Variety button holes." This agrees with Lt Munson Hoy's surviving coat in the Connecticut Historical Society, which is scarlet with dark blue collar, cuffs and lapels, white turnbacks, gold buttons and lace.

D2: Officer, North Carolina Volunteers, c.1780–83

The 1783 New York List mentions "Red Coat – Plain Blue Lappel" for this regiment. Red coats, but with no facing or button colors, are indicated in Wiederhold's 1783 Ms Almanack. The facings are confirmed by the surviving coat of Capt John Legget, which is scarlet with dark blue collar, cuffs and lapels, gold buttons (stamped with crowned "RP"), square-ended gold lace buttonholes set in pairs, gold epaulettes and white turnbacks. It thus seems that the officers indulged in lace while the men's buttonholes were plain. (Collection of the Public Archives of Nova Scotia, Halifax)

D3: 84th Foot, Royal Highland Emigrants, 1777–84

The Highland-style red coats faced with blue with the "Highland part of the Cloathing, viz. plaids and tartans" first went to the 2nd Bn in Halifax in late 1776; part of this clothing was sent on to Québec and issued to the 1st Bn in mid-1777. On July 4 that year the men were ordered to "make the half plaids lately given out into a kilt and three pairs of hose." For their march to Sorel in August they were "to have on Little Kilts of the Regimental Plaid, Hose of the same and Red garters." There was plenty of plaid for the 1st Bn thereafter: Col MacLean wrote in 1780 that "plaid and tartans, we have in great abundance." By 1782 the kilts had obviously worn out, since they had been turned into "Plad Trousers"

Brass cartridge box plate, Butler's Rangers. (Musée du Château de Ramezay, Montréal; author's photo)

and "tartan trousers" – in effect, trews had been made out of the kilts. New kilts were not issued; by May 1784 "Breeches in lieu of half plaid" were being issued to the men, shortly before the 1st Bn was disbanded in June (LAC, MG23, K1/27 and 30).

Like the 1st Bn in Québec, the 2nd Bn in Halifax did not receive at once the uniform of red faced with blue and the Government tartan plaid. In September 1775 the 2nd Bn's recruits in Halifax were to be dressed in what was available: "a westcoat [sic] of spotted swan skin, light infantry fashion, with sleeves of the same, white breeches of coarse thick stockings, blue leggings, that will come up near the crotch, and garters of red tape below the knee ... a blanket coat overall with a Canadian cap ... and their old hats trimmed in neatest manner as can." Mittens were of a "white milled kind of cloth." The "Highland part of the Cloathing, viz. plaids and tartans" apparently still had not reached the 2nd Bn in Halifax by the end of June 1776 (CO 5/168); but it did arrive in the fall, and part of this clothing was then sent on to Québec for the 1st Battalion. Grenadiers were intended to have match cases – a list of items to be shipped included "106 matches & Rings, 106 match Cases"; while the light infantrymen got "Hatchet with Cases," and everybody had "Broad swords" issued, for which scabbards were made in 1777 (T 64/115). The 2nd Bn must have looked splendid when its colors were consecrated and presented at Halifax in July 1777 (NY Gazette, July 7, 1777). All this Highland regalia impressed Andrew Sherburne, a stranded American sailor, who recalled being taken into custody by a party of the 84th "in their kilts, plaids, Scotch bonnets, and checkered stockings, accoutred with guns and fixt bayonets, broad swords, &c. I had seen the like before in Charleston, S.C." Generally speaking, the 2nd Bn seems to have managed to dress in Highland uniform until its disbandment.

E1: Queen's Loyal Rangers, 1777–78

This unit was initially clothed in red faced with green: in May 1778, a servant ran away wearing "a red coat faced with green, buff waistcoat and breeches, and an old blanket coat" (*Québec Gazette*, May 21, 1778). It was issued blue coats faced with white from about late 1778; but from 1780 it had green coats faced with red.

E2: King's Loyal Americans, 1778–80

The first regimentals for "Jessups and followers" were "the cheapest that could be got at Montréal, very common Red stuff turned up with green, as Red seemed to be their favorite colour," wrote Maj Grey to Governor Carleton on January 12, 1777. This uniform was probably laced, as "trimmings" were also mentioned. The King's Loyal Americans received blue coats faced with white in late 1778, and the similarity to those worn by many American patriot units raised protests – see above. The unit was issued green coats faced with red from about 1780–81 (Add Mss 21,818, 21,821). The issue of blue coats faced with white was not unique to Canada: in Jamaica, the Duke of Cumberland's Regt had "a short blue jacket with white facings" in 1781–82, according to the American sailor Ebenizer Fox.

E3: Loyal Rangers (Jessup's), 1782–84

This unit, formed from several small Loyalist corps in Canada in November 1781, was issued in February 1782 with green coats faced with red, shirts, stockings, hats and moccasins (Add Mss 21849). A silver button in the Canadian War Museum collections, engraved "Rangers," with a crown above and wreath around, is associated with this unit.

F1: 3rd Battalion, New Jersey Volunteers, c.1779–83

According to the 1777 List the first uniform was green. This is confirmed by a description of men from the unit taken prisoner by the Americans as dressed in "a green coat, white waistcoat and breeches" when they escaped in December 1777 (*Pennsylvania Packet*, December 24, 1777). The unit "changed their green coats for red ones" in about May 1778 (*New Jersey Gazette*, June 17, 1778). In March 1780, new uniforms were described in an American intelligence report as "Scarlet Coats Trimmed with Blue, Jackets and Breeches White." The 1783 New York List mentions, for the 1st Bn, "Red Coat – Blue Lappel White button hole – button Equal Distance"; for the 2nd Bn the same, but "buttons near each other in Pairs – for Distinction"; and for the 3rd Bn the buttons "close together by threes." Wiederhold's 1783 Ms Almanack lists red coats faced with blue, and silver buttons for officers. This last description agrees with a half-length portrait of Maj Robert Drummond, 2nd Bn, showing him wearing a scarlet coat with blue collar and lapels, silver buttons set in pairs, buttonholes trimmed with narrow silver lace, silver epaulette and white waistcoat (Haarmann, *JSAHR*, 1971). An officer's silvered shoulder belt plate bearing the crowned royal cipher with "New Jersey Volunteers" is at Upper Canada Village (Morrisburg, Ontario). The rank and file may have had the same in brass.

F2: Drummer, 3rd Battalion, De Lancey's Brigade, c.1781–83

The early uniform was green (1777 List). In March 1779 a deserter was described as wearing "a cocked hat, silver laced, a regimental coat lapelled with green, and a blue surtout coat" – the coat appears to have been changed to red by then, as in many other Loyalist units. Drummers in the British forces wore "reversed" coats, i.e. of the facing color; so did those of Loyalist units, but they do not usually seem to have been issued bearskin caps. A surviving 1782 bill specifies green cloth for making drummers' and fifers' coats for De Lancey's 3rd Bn (LAC, MG 23, D1/24), which agrees with the uniform of red faced with green, with silver buttons for officers, mentioned in Wiederhold's 1783 Almanack. The 1783 New York List gives differences for the first two battalions: 1st Bn, "Red Coat – Plain Blue Lappel"; 2nd Bn, the same blue facings but "buttons Double Distance in Pairs" on the coat. The 3rd Bn may therefore have had buttons grouped in threes, as was the fashion of the time. We show the drummer's coat without lace, since the 1782 bill does not mention buttonhole lace for the regiment.

F3: Officer, Volunteers of Ireland, c.1779–83

The uniform of this unit is not described in any of the lists, neither are the colors given in clothing invoices of 1780 and

Officer's silver shoulder belt plate, Queen's Rangers, c.1780. The unit of the same title that served in Upper Canada 1791–1802 may also have used this pattern. (Parks Canada)

1781, except to mention that the men's waistcoats and breeches were white (PRO 30/55/3419, 9904). The invoices do mention that all enlisted men had caps, not hats, and that the caps of the sergeants were ornamented with silver. The 1782 invoices at last mention "Red Coats; Green Brandenburg [laced button] holes White Waistcoat & breeches," surely meant for this unit (PRO 30/55/4307). The Volunteers also had "Trowsers," and even some mitts, according to an issue of January 1783 (WO 1/13). An engraving of the colonel of the regiment, Lord Rawdon, shows him wearing a coatee with wide "Brandenburg"-style laces with tassels, and a collar edged with lacing; this is the only Loyalist provincial unit known to have had such a uniform. A cartouche below the portrait shows small figures of soldiers wearing caps and coatees, which would obviously be men of his unit (print from *American Heritage Book of the Revolution*, 1958, p.333). Our figure is a reconstruction of the likely appearance of an officer of this unit according to the data cited above. The general style of the short-tailed coatee, notably the pointed cuffs, is consistent with the fashions of the period. Silver lace and buttons have been chosen, because of the reference to silver on the sergeant's caps, bearing in mind that this could also simply be a distinction peculiar to NCOs.

G1: Trooper, British Legion, c.1781–83

The early dress of Tarleton's cavalrymen appears to have consisted of green jackets, green waistcoats, green plush breeches and red cloaks; and that for his infantrymen of green jackets, black stocks, white waistcoats and breeches. The jacket was described in 1780 as a "light green waistcoat, without skirts, with black cuffs and capes [collars], and nothing more." Lists of clothing sent in 1780 mention "Green jackets & Waistcoats Laced" and some buckskin breeches, these last probably for the cavalrymen; and in 1781, green jackets and waistcoats and white breeches, with no mention of lace. The clothing sent in 1782 was described as "Green Light Infantry Coats, & Jackets, Black Collars & Cuffs, White Breeches." This generally agrees with the 1783 New York List's description, which has, for the Legion's cavalry, "Short Round Green Tight Jacketts, Black Cuff & Collar," and for the infantry, "Short Coat – Green with Same Lappel, Variety Button hole & Black Cuff & Collar." Officers appear initially to have worn "short green Coats trimmed with narrow Gold Lace," according to a 1780 description of two captured officers of the Legion who escaped their American gaolers. In about 1782 black collars and cuffs were added to the officer's uniform. Tarleton's full-length portrait of 1782 by Sir Joshua Reynolds shows him in a green jacket with black collar and cuffs, gold lace and buttons (see page 10). A miniature of Tarleton made that same year shows him in a green dress coat with black collar and lapels (and no doubt the cuffs also) with gold buttons, no lace, and gold epaulettes. Wiederhold's 1783 Almanack correctly gives the corps green coats faced with black, but mentions silver buttons for officers instead of gold – obviously an error. The British Legion was reported "mostly clad in white" when campaigning in the Carolinas and Virginia during 1780–81, according to Simcoe's journal. The trooper shown here is based on the above documents and a background figure shown on Tarleton's 1782 portrait.

G2: Officer, Queen's Rangers, c.1781–83

When the corps was raised in 1776 the Queen's Rangers' uniform was green. However, in the spring of 1778 the authorities determined to "Cloth the Provincials" in red, a color ill-suited for Rangers, so that "Major Simcoe exerted himself to preserve the [Queen's] Rangers in green, and to procure them green waistcoats; his purpose was to wear the waistcoats with their sleeves during the campaign, and to add sleeves to the shell or outer coat, to be worn over the waistcoat in winter; green is without comparison the best colour for light troops with dark accoutrements, and if put on in the spring, in autumn it nearly fades with the leaves, preserving its characteristic of being scarcely visible at a distance" (Simcoe's *Journal*). Thus, although reported in red uniforms in the 1777 list, the Queen's Rangers in fact remained clothed in green. As can be seen in the illustrations (see pages 16–19), the unit assumed different styles of dress as it grew into a larger, legion-sized corps. Loyalist Highlanders joined the corps as its 11th Company on October 20, 1777, and "the command of it given to Captain McKay. They were furnished with the Highland dress and their national piper." Up to 1780 the Queen's Rangers mostly wore hats, but caps were issued from that year; the various types of companies mostly had black caps with a white metal crescent. Following the execution of Major André by the Americans in October 1780, Simcoe ordered that "the regiment should immediately be provided with black and white feather" as a sign of mourning. Surviving shipment records from 1780 to 1782 mention green jackets and light infantry coats, white waistcoats, breeches and trousers, and caps with ornaments. The New York 1783 List mentions, for the cavalry: "Short Green round Jacketts – black Cuff & Collar – with Plain Black Cloth Hussar Caps – Momento Front"; and for the infantry, "Green Short Coats, Lappel Same, Black Cuff & Collar." Wiederhold's 1783 Almanack has green coats faced with green, and silver buttons for officers. Surviving officers' portraits and garments show that black facings were probably adopted toward the end of the war. Colonel Simcoe's half-length portrait shows a green coat with green collar and black lapels. Captain William Jarvis' coat (see opposite) was for dress occasions and, from the style of its collar, may date from c.1785 or somewhat later, to be used by an officer on half-pay; nevertheless, it provides excellent information on the officer's dress at the end of the war. It shows black velvet facings at the collar, cuffs and lapels, the silver lace being set in the wavy "teardrop" fashion ending in a point. Jarvis wears this coat in his c.1791 portrait, and Capts Saunders and Smith wear similar coats (except for a lower collar for Saunders) in their c.1790 portraits. The officer shown here is a composite reconstruction from surviving garments and images.

G3: King's American Dragoons, 1781–83

This unit was "to be clothed, armed & accoutred as near as possible like the Regiments of Light Dragoons on the British establishment" (PRO 30/55/2812). The 1783 New York List described its dress as: "Red Short Coat – Helmeted Caps – Blue Lappels Variety button hole." Wiederhold's 1783 Almanack mentioned red coats faced with blue, and gold buttons for officers. Clothing sent to the corps included helmets, forage caps, coats, waistcoats, breeches, rifle shirts, trousers, blue greatcoats, stocks, gloves, swords, pistols, carbines with bayonets, accoutrements and saddlery (PRO 30/55/10278). The unit also bought "Scarlet looping for helmets" (LAC, RG9, C1901), and blue "Watering" jackets, white waistcoats and leather breeches in 1783 (LAC, MG23, D1/24). Our reconstruction of a dismounted trooper includes the "Tarleton" helmet as the most likely headdress, probably with a red turban. The lace is shown evenly spaced, although it may have been in pairs, especially for officers. The blue greatcoat is rolled on the knapsack.

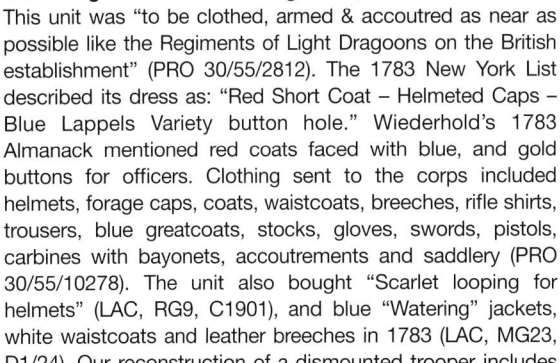

H1: Officer, King's American Regiment, c.1780–83

The uniform of this unit appears always to have been red. It is given that color in the 1777 List; and in the 1783 New York List we find "Red Coat, Olive Lappel, Variety button hole." However, in Wiederhold's 1783 Almanack the facing color is listed as blue, with gold buttons for officers. This agrees with the c.1780–83 portrait of Ensign E. Budd, preserved at Fort Malden National Historic Site at Amherstburg, Ontario, which shows the coat facings as being plain, without buttonhole lace. A gilded gorget to this unit with a scroll bearing "The King's American Regiment," and a gilded officer's rectangular shoulder belt plate with similar markings, are recorded (*JSAHR*, 1923; Todd Albums, Anne S.K. Brown Military Collection, Brown University).

H2: Loyal American Rangers (Oddell's), 1781–83

In September 1782, Gideon White in New York wrote to LtCol Oddell in Jamaica asking if the corp's uniform was "green and black or red and green" – the answer is regrettably missing (Public Archives of Nova Scotia, White Coll, Vol.2), but it was probably red faced with green. During 1782 a supply of uniforms for "Provincial Forces in Jamaica" included "Red Light Infantry Coats, Linen Linings, Green Facings, White Lace, White Waistcoat & Breeches," with "Light Infantry Caps," for a battalion of 516 privates, and this was almost certainly intended for the Loyal American Rangers (T 27/34).

H3: South Carolina Royalists/Carolina Corps, c.1782–84

This was probably the appearance of both white and black soldiers in the South Carolina Royalists, and of the black soldiers of the Carolina Corps. Wiederhold's 1783 Almanack states that the South Carolina Royalists had red coats, but no facing and button colors are indicated. Fortunately, the 1783 New York List mentions "Red Coat — Yellow Lappel Variety button hole," with, presumably, white metal buttons, white turnbacks, waistcoat and breeches for the South Carolina Royalists. The black soldiers formed into the Carolina Corps and sent to Grenada in 1783 probably continued to wear the regiment's uniform.

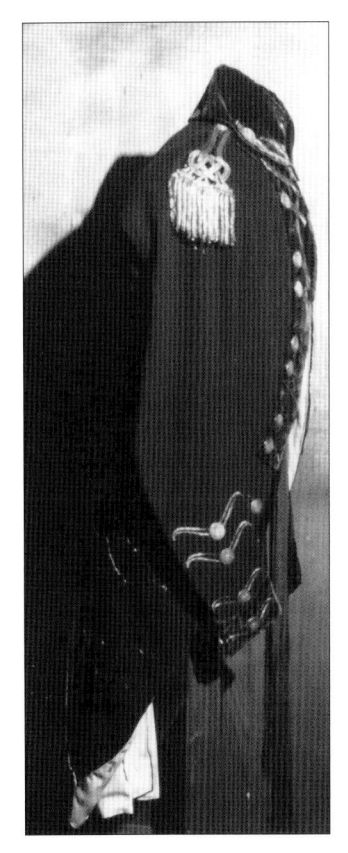

Dress coat of Capt William Jarvis, Queen's Rangers, c.1785 – the only known surviving garment associated with this unit. Dark green with black velvet collar, cuffs and lapels, white turnbacks, silver buttons, silver "teardrop" curved lace ending in a point, and silver epaulettes. The collar is of slightly "raised and fall" shape, an emerging fashion in the 1780s. Note the sleeve buttons set between two opposed "teardrops" in "herringbone" fashion; the skirt buttons and lace are also set on in this way. (Old Fort York, Toronto; author's photos)

INDEX

Figures in **bold** refer to illustrations.

1st American Regiment 15
2nd American Regiment 17
5th American Regiment 11
105th Foot 17

American Legion 10
American States (1777–78) **5**
American Volunteers 10
Amherst's Corps 33
Armed Boatmen 10
Artificers 17
Artificers & Labourers (Newfoundland) 22
Associated Loyalists 10

Bahamas Loyal Volunteers 33–34
Barbadian Rangers 34
Barrack Master General's Volunteers 37
Batteaumen 17
belt plate **15**
Black Corps of Dragoons, Pioneers and Artificers 34
Black Dragoons 10
Black Pioneers 10
Boston militias 37
Brant, Joseph **6**
British Legion 10–11, **13**
Buck's County Light Dragoons 11
Butler's Rangers 17–18, **21**

Caledonian Volunteers 11
camp of Loyalists at Johnstown **40**
Canada 17–22
Canadian Companies 18
Carolina Corps 34
Carolinas militias 38
Central America and West Indies 33–36
Charleston Loyal Militia 38
Chester County Light Dragoons 11
chronology 7–9
Claus, Daniel 22

De Lancey's Brigade 11
De Lancey's Refugees 11
Detroit Volunteers 18
Diemar's Hussars 11
Duke of Cumberland's Regiment 34

East Florida Rangers 24
Emmerich's Chasseurs 11
Engineer Volunteers 37
Ethiopian Regiment 11

Fanning, Col Edmund 14
Ferguson's Detachment 10
Florida 24, 33
French, Lt Jeremiah 33, 34, 35

Garrison Battalion 34–35
Georgia Light Dragoons 11
Georgia Loyalists 11
Guides & Pioneers 12

Hierlihy's Corps of Independent Companies 22–23
Highland Volunteers 37

Independent Companies (Mosquito Coast) 35
Indian Department 18–19

Jamaica Legion 35
Jamaica Volunteers 35–36
Jarvis, Capt William 47

King's American Dragoons 12
    standard of **1**
King's American Regiment 12
    belt plate **15**

King's Dock Yard Volunteers 37
King's Loyal Americans 19
King's Orange Rangers 23
King's Rangers 12
King's Rangers (Rogers') 20
King's Royal Regiment of New York 20

Lancey, Col James de **3**
Langlade, Michel Mouet de 24
Leake's Corps 20
Lewis' Corps of Light Dragoons 36
Loyal American Associators 37
Loyal American Rangers 36
Loyal American Regiment 12
Loyal Foresters 12
Loyal Irish Volunteers 37
Loyal King's County Militia 38
Loyal New Englanders 12
Loyal Newport Associators 12
Loyal Queen's County Militia 38
Loyal Rangers (Jessup's) 21
Loyal Refugee Volunteers 38
Loyal Rhode Islanders 12
Loyal Suffolk Militia 38
Loyal Westchester Volunteers 38
Loyalists **40**

McKay's Corps 21
Marine Artillery 37
Maryland Loyalists 12
Massachusetts Volunteer Company 37–38
Military Batteaumen 24
militias 36–38
Mosquito Shore Volunteers 36

Nassau Blues 13
Natchez Volunteers 24
Naudière, Charles Tarrieu de La **38**
New Hampshire Volunteers 16
Newfoundland and Nova Scotia 22–24
Newfoundland Regiment 23
New Jersey Volunteers 13
New York City militias 37
New York Rangers 13, 37
New York Volunteer Rifle Company 13
New York Volunteers 13, 37
Nicaragua **5**
North Carolina Highland Regiment 13–14
North Carolina Independent Company 14
North Carolina Independent Dragoons 14
North Carolina Light Dragoons 14
North Carolina Militia 38
North Carolina Volunteers 14
Nova Scotia and Newfoundland 22–24
Nova Scotia militias 37
Nova Scotia Volunteers 23

Ordnance Loyal Volunteers 37

Pennsylvania Loyalists 14
Philadelphia Light Dragoons 14
Prince of Wales' American Regiment 14
Provincial Light Infantry 14
Provincial Marine 21

Québec militias 37
Queen's Loyal Rangers 22
Queen's Own Loyal Virginia Regiment 15
Queen's Rangers 15
    troops of **16, 17, 18**

Roman Catholic Volunteers 15
Royal American Reformees 15
Royal Batteaux Corps 36
Royal Bergen Volunteers 37
Royal Fencible Americans 23
Royal Foresters 15

Royal Georgia Volunteers 15–16
Royal Highland Emigrants 22, 23–24
    camp color **36**
Royal North British Volunteers 37
Royal North Carolina Volunteers 14

St. John's Island Volunteers 24
Salaberry, Lt Louis de **20**
Sandford's Troop of Provincial Cavalry 16
Simcoe, Col John Graves 19
South Carolina Light Dragoons 16
South Carolina Rangers 16
South Carolina Royalists 16
Starckloff's Light Dragoons 16
Stark's Corps 16
Staten Island Troop of Light Horse 16
Stewart's Light Dragoons 16
Stewart's Provincial Light Dragoons 16
Stewart's Troop of Guides and Expresses 16

Tarleton, LtCol Banastre 10
Thayeadanegea **6**
Turks & Caicos Islands 36

uniforms
    belt insignia **15, 43, 44, 46**
    box insignia **44, 45**
    British Legion **10, 13, G1** (31, 46)
    Butler's Rangers **21, C3** (27, 44)
    button designs **41, 42**
    Canadian Companies 20
    De Lancey's Brigade **F2** (30, 45)
    Ethiopian Regiment **A2** (25, 42)
    Indian Department **22, 23, 24, C1** (27, 43)
    King's American Dragoons **G3** (31, 47)
    King's American Regiment **14, H1** (32, 47)
    King's Loyal Americans **E2** (29, 45)
    King's Royal Regiment 33, 34, 35
    King's Royal Regiment of New York **C2** (27, 43–44)
    Loyal American Associators **A1** (25, 42)
    Loyal American Rangers (Oddell's) **H2** (32, 47)
    Loyal Ranger's (Jessup's) **E3** (29, 45)
    New Jersey Volunteers **F1** (30, 45)
    North Carolina Volunteers **D2** (28, 44)
    Oliver De Lancey's Brigade **3**
    Prince of Wales' American Regiment **D1** (28, 44)
    privates **4, 16, 18, 19, B3** (26, 43), **39**
    Québec City Militia **B1** (26, 43), **38**
    Queen's Loyal Rangers **E1** (29, 45)
    Queen's Rangers **16, 17, 18, 19, G2** (31, 46–47), **47**
    Royal Fencible Americans **A3** (25, 42–43)
    Royal Highland Emigrants **B2** (26, 43), **D3** (28, 44–45)
    South Carolina Royalists **H3** (32, 47)
    Volunteers of Ireland **F3** (30, 45–46)
Union flag **6**
United Corps of Pennsylvania & Maryland Loyalists 24, 33

Volunteers of Ireland 16–17
Volunteers of New England 16
Vrooman, Sgt Adam **21**

Wentworth's Regiment 17
West Florida Loyal Refugees 33
West Florida Provincial Regiment 33
West Florida Royal Foresters 33
West Indies and Central America 33–36
West Jersey Volunteers 17
Westchester Light Horse 11
Wilmington Light Dragoons 14

Young's Company 36